Lee Tae-Sang is a journalist/columnist and a published author of twenty-four books. He translated Kahlil Gibran's *The Prophet, The Garden of the Prophet, Spirits Rebellious, Nymphs of the Valley,* and Thomas Mann's *Transposed Heads* into Korean. He has worked within the publishing industry in both Korea and England and is the founder of the online newspaper, *Cosmian News*. He studied Philosophy and Religion and has owned several businesses.

As a court interpreter for the city of New York for the past seventeen years, he has found the ideal place to reflect on the path of his unpredictable, global life and observe the present human condition.

To my grandchildren:
Elijah, Theodore, and Julia.

Lee Tae-Sang

COSMIAN

AUSTIN MACAULEY PUBLISHERS™

LONDON · CAMBRIDGE · NEW YORK · SHARJAH

Ordering Information:
Quantity sales: special discounts are available on quantity purchases by corporations, associations, and others. For details, contact the publisher at the address below.

Publisher's Cataloging-in-Publication data
Lee, Tae-Sang
Cosmian

ISBN 9781643784816 (Paperback)
ISBN 9781643784823 (Hardback)
ISBN 9781645367925 (ePub e-book)

Library of Congress Control Number: 2019908491

The main category of the book — BIOGRAPHY & AUTOBIOGRAPHY / Personal Memoirs.

www.austinmacauley.com/us

First Published (2019)
Austin Macauley Publishers LLC
40 Wall Street, 28th Floor
New York, NY 10005
USA

mail-usa@austinmacauley.com
+1 (646) 5125767

Table of Contents

Preface

All of us, born on this star called the planet earth to leave after a short stay, each living with whatever kind of love, in whatever style of life, in whatever color, shape, and form, in one's own way, each can say something special for one sentence, as different from each other. And yet if we were to find one common denominator, could it not be that 'we all are Cosmians?' So on this proposition that 'we all are Cosmians,' I am inviting each one of you to share that sentence of yours. Each will be the song of a pearl-like life, or rather of a rainbow-like love.

'Cosmian' is one of two newly coined words by me and the other one is *'Arainbow.'* That is to be right on the rainbow itself, instead of just beholding or pursuing it.

Cosmian News, a daily, global online newspaper, was launched on July 10th, 2018, in Seoul, Korea. Its mission is to enlighten, inspire and uplift us all, regardless of nationality, race, sex, etc.; to realize that each and every one of us is a 'seeker' on one's own cosmic journey; and to turn our chaotic world into the cosmos of harmony, love and peace. To be such an aspiring Cosmian is to be Arainbow. So let's all be *Cosmians Arainbow*.

"If each one of us is indeed a micro-cosmos reflecting a macro-cosmos, all that existed in the past, all that exists at present and all that will exist in the future, we're all in it together, all on our separate journeys to realize this. May every one of us be the sea of cosmos!"

– quoted from Mr. Lee Tae-Sang's book ***Cosmos Cantata*** *(Mayhaven Publishing, Inc. 2013)*

Foreword

Success and Luck: Good Fortune and The Myth of Meritocracy by Robert H. Frank, which came out in 2017, was recently translated and published in Korean, entitled 'To the Successful by the Virtue of Competence and Endeavor.'

In this book, the author, a professor of economics at Cornell University, argues that the successful tend to underestimate the role that chance plays. The issue is whether hard work or luck that decides the outcome of success. This may sound like there's no other option, but I'd like to present the third option one can take. Whatever and how many options there are, what you decide to take is up to your choice. Isn't it?

All the while living my life for eighty-two years, I've never even dreamed that there would be a day like today, one day. Looking back, had I not lost my first love almost sixty years ago, I could not have come to realize that I and all others, all beings, were 'cosmians' born 'arainbow' from the Cosmos. A young boy who happened to fall in love with the microcosmos of a flower ended up embracing the whole macrocosmos.

Although everyone encounters, from time to time, both blessings and curses in disguise, doesn't it make all the difference depending, no matter whether it's a 'fortune' or a 'misfortune,' on what one makes it to be, after all? We see all the time the fall of the most powerful and successful from the pinnacle of power and success, while some 'hopeless' and 'helpless' losers rise from the ashes of despair and failures, like a phoenix.

I'd like to share a bit of my most recent experience. In September of 2017, two books "*39 Project*" and "*Tae-Mi Sa-Byun*" were published and appeared on The Recommended List of Books for Readers in Their Twenties in Korea. "*39 Project*" is an essay collection by 39 creative, free-spirited, trailblazing young people. "*Tae-Mi*" (a combination of the first names of the co-authors, namely Lee T<u>ae</u>-Sang and Kim M<u>i</u>-Rae) "*Sa-Byun*" (meaning Dialectic Dialogue) has the subtitle '*Thought Romance Between An 80-Year-Old Man and A 24-Year-Old Girl.*' I commissioned this very promising young entrepreneur who had pulled off these two great surprise feats of publishing success to launch a new quarterly 'Cosmian' in the same spirit and vein of the now defunct, very popular intellectual monthly magazine 'Ssassanggye' (meaning The World of Thoughts) in March, 2018. Although this project was aborted, it was replaced by another much more meaningful and visionary global online daily newspaper, The Cosmian News *http://www.cosmiannews.com.*

In 2018, my Korean publisher, Ms. Jeon Seungseon, Poet, Novelist, and Playwright, started writing a nonfiction narrative of my life, 'Cosmian' (in Korean), and it was published on June 1, 2018. So I contacted Ms. Deborah Smith, the English translator of Korean novelist Han Kang's novel 'The Vegetarian,' which won The Man Booker International Prize in 2016. Since my approach was unsuccessful, I decided to translate it into English myself, revising and rewriting it in my own words.

Furthermore, a Cosmian Festival in celebration of the inauguration of The Cosmian News was held in Seoul, Korea, on October 27, 2018. On October 19, 2019, the First Cosmian Prize will be awarded to the top two non-fiction narrative essay contest winners with 7 million won (Korean currency, equivalent to about $7,000) for the grand prize and 3 million won for the gold prize. The Second Cosmian Festival will take place in Pyongchang, Korea, in the fall of 2020, on the campus of Cosmian University at its inauguration, Cosmos willing. Cosmian University may include Cosmian School of Music and Cosmian Orchestra, again Cosmos willing.

I do agree with Buddha:

"With our thoughts, we make the world."

A new album, *Cosmian Song: As Heart Beats* by Korean singer-songwriter, Navid, popular in China, Japan, and Korea, was issued on June 30, 2019. The lyrics of the title song of the album was written by Ms. Jeon Seungseon.

Therefore, as the saying goes, if not this, someone or something far better will turn up, sooner or later, if one never ceases to look for what one wants. I'm reminded of a comment confided by the late V. S. Naipaul (1932–2018), winner of the 2001 Nobel Prize for Literature, who was born in Trinidad in a family with Indian roots and just passed away. *"I knew the door I wanted. I knocked."*

He must have meant to say that there are many doors. If one door doesn't open, I'll knock another. If another door still doesn't, I'll knock yet another, until one opens.

At the same time, we'd better recall Steve Jobs' motto: *"The journey (itself) is the reward."*

It is tough to accept the hard truths of life but we all have to accept them anyway. One is that for anything to happen anytime anywhere, the whole Cosmos has to conspire. Won't it be?

Anyway, I concur with Toni Morrison:

"At some point in life world's beauty becomes enough."

Chapter I
This Is Life

I'm getting ready to end my visit to earth. It's about time to get off the roller coaster of life on this planet and resume my cosmic journey. Now in my eighties, life to me has been an amazing, mysterious, and wonderful game. Although I don't know on whose invitation I came, I came without an inkling of how I came here, but I've lived with all my heart and soul, loving every moment to the fullest. I can now confess that the source of the love I felt for each breath was the Lady of my life.

I am going to meet her. In order to meet the Lady who gave me death and then gave life back to me, I packed my travel bag. I'm going to enjoy 'coming home.' Come to think of it, I started my life with an adventure and I am ending it with an adventure. It's the miracle of miracles that I can still remember her. I believe that a miracle is what happens that has to happen.

For my trip to Seoul, I got a leave for ten days from my job working as a New York State court interpreter. My colleagues wished me a very happy bon voyage that might be my last one. They have been curious about my motherland, about the roots of my thoughts, and about the love of my life.

I named the Ladies Cosmians. It's time to give them my 'thanksgiving.' It's time to confess my love for them in the most beautiful words of life. As all things that came to me turned into love, I need to come to them and be the love for them. I've finally arrived at a critical point of meeting all the Ladies in the Universe of Love to love them all eternally.

I put in my bag a copy of my book, *'Ode to Life,'* which just came out. After receiving copies of this book from my publisher, I was talking to myself: Time was for me to look out for the Lady. *'Ode to Life'* was my lifelong song sung for the Lady, never aging in my memory. Had I not met her on this picnic on earth, my journey as a speck of cosmic dust would have been dull and meaningless.

I know the Lady and I will never vanish, even if I can dredge up all my egos from the swamp of sensations caused by my fickle body. As the river never stops flowing and the ocean never dries up, we'll never cease to be. As the sea and waves are the same, as clay and pottery are one, she and I are one and the same. I know my longing for her will never stop till my last breath is taken away. This longing is the synonym of love. Love is Life. Love is Creation. The Lady is Love, Life, and Creation.

At the least, the Lady was the beginning and the end of the knowledge, far beyond what one sought.

As long as the sun was rising in the morning and the stars were twinkling at night, while the flowers were blooming in the spring and the leaves were falling in the autumn, life was full of wonder and nothing but blessings

16

for me. The Lady was like the sun and the stars to me. Yes, indeed, she was a Cosmian who came to me arainbow. It took a long time for me to be aware of this mystery.

Watching me packing up to leave, my ten-year-old grandson Elijah shrugged his shoulders and sighed: "This is life!" Then he walked away with a soccer ball.

After he left, I tried to recall when I was at his age. Seoul back then remained only in my distant memory as a faded black and white picture, and it will be no longer there. This thought almost made me repeat what Elijah said: "This Is Life!"

Yes, 'This Is Life!' Otherwise, the Ladies couldn't be there. I'll be departing from JFK Airport tomorrow morning to look for them.

When I finished packing, it was night already. I closed my eyes. Time was exiting my body, or rather I was running out of time. I felt like I ascended from the earthly realm into an unworldly one. Maybe time doesn't pass or stop. I may be passing and stopping, instead. Falling half-asleep I started seeing images. As if I was dreaming in a dream, I was reciting a poem I had composed years ago while walking along the Hudson River.

I've got to love death so that I can love life.
As there can be cosmos because of chaos,
These two are twins.

Day and Night,
Life and Death,
Joy and Sorrow,
Generosity and Greed,

Understanding and Anger,
Wisdom and Ignorance.

These two are two and one,
Like Cosmos and Chaos.
These two are Siamese Twins.

Chapter II
Time Travel

Lightly kicking off the ground, the plane was soaring up into the sky, pushing back JFK Airport behind. The sky was as blue and clear like my grandson Elijah's eyes. Born of a Hebrew dad and a Korean mom, Elijah has mysteriously beautiful blue eyes. Looking at Elijah's eyes, I often thought that the universe must be emitting endlessly waves of blue light through his eyes, as intense as in the sky.

With my eyes closed I was time traveling, enjoying the slight sensation seeping through my body by the flight of the plane. I was a traveler, and at the same time the travel itself. Or rather, I was time itself. Time was not taking me back to the past. I was looking at time from outside of time.

I was looking at my present self from my past self. I could tell that the word eternity meant nothing to me. The carefree childhood, the passionate youth, and the peaceful old age, they were all the same state of mind, always there, never changing, like Polaris. It was my mind, minding them, that's been changed. I sauntered into time to visit my past self.

"Excuse me. May I offer you a drink? Orange juice, or something else?" a flight attendant asked me.

"Just water, please. Thank you."

With a smile, the attendant poured water into my glass. Sipping water, I looked out the window. The plane was flying above the clouds. It seemed like I was riding a carriage on the cotton quilt seat that was covering the whole globe. I am presently over the clouds, and mere a fleck of dirt. No, not even that, must I be, less than a grain of dust, the infinitesimal particle. I could be reduced to nothing, from which I might have emerged particle by particle.

Hours passed and the plane was sailing like a sailboat, pulled by time and space. Passengers had fallen asleep; it was all quiet. I wasn't thinking about anything. No thoughts entered my mind, to be exact. I was feeling the motion of the plane simply being drawn into time and space. To be free of thoughts and feelings might be to be weightless in a gravity-free state, as when you were in love. I thought I had heard the Lady's voice coming out of no-where and no-when, channeling probably through my unconsciousness, and even possibly through my sub- or super-consciousness.

"Tae-Sang, we are not short of time. Like water springs endlessly, it wells up out of eternity. So let's not worry about it."

I was floating freely within myself and I moved where her voice was coming from. Her illusory image was pulling me back to the past. As she said, I might have saved the infinite time for nothing while squandering the finite time allotted to me.

"Oh, you were there all the time, like time itself!"

"Yes, Tae-Sang, as always you were there. I, too, was here all the time. So please don't be anxious. Just shine your light to me. We'll be connected and inseparable forever. That's how we become one."

She was the one whom I longed for all my life, and it was she who let me know that the fairer sex was my religion, the beginning and ending of my universe. I never had a doubt about this truth. Love was her name. No man could exist without her. Life was meaningless without her. From her I got life, and I was living because of her.

From the sea of love, one by one, all my dear Ladies were recalled. All the longings were like the fragrance of flowers. It was everywhere. Really and truly, life was so fragile and yet so magical. Ever since my youngest days, I've had so much fun, enjoying the game of life, moment by moment, in the most exciting and thrilling playground called the world, where everything was a toy. There was nothing to throw away. In the not-distant future, my stay here on earth will come to end and I will be traveling on my cosmic flight to another star. Wherever I go, my Lady will always be my 'homecoming.'

The plane is flying over the Pacific Ocean now. With my eyes still closed, I am time traveling to her.

Chapter III

The First Lady, Mother
She, the Mother, Is the Light

When I was five, she became a widow at the age of 45, as mother of 15 children—12 of her own and 3 stepchildren born of her late husband's first wife, who had died young.

She fell in love with the teacher of her younger brother while acting as his absent-father-substitute, since their father had left for Manchuria, involved in independence movement fighting against Japanese Imperial colonial rule of Korea. She was one of the very few high-school-educated young ladies in the country in those days.

She was the first love of my life, the beginning, and the ending of humanity and of creation. Born of a sperm from my dad and of an egg from my mom, each originating from one of each, going back ad infinitum, I am one with the wind, the sun, and the stars. There is nothing that is not me.

The revival of womankind full of care, charity, grace, nobility, and sanctity is visited upon us through motherhood. My dad and his dad and his dad all came through motherhood. Taking on all the world's pains and worries, our mother raised us singlehanded. Sorrow and despair couldn't approach her and kept away from her.

My dad was born posthumously to a family that had only one child each for three consecutive generations. He loved all children, not just his own. He published a children's book entitled *Children's Paradise*, a collection of poems, songs, and plays he had written for children. It was written in Korean, when the Korean language was banned by the Japanese, who occupied Korea for 35 years until the end of World War II. Under the Japanese rule, Korean people lost not only their language and culture, but also their names and identities when they were forced to give up their Korean names and adopt Japanese ones, instead. Of the 500 copies printed, the one copy of *Children's Paradise* my father had kept at home was lost during the Korean War.

I read the book when I first learned to read. I do not remember the exact wording of one poem "Goldfish," but I do remember the essence of the poem. It was about a child talking to himself on a rainy day, looking at a goldfish in a bowl.

Goldfish

Always happy at play swimming
Around and around
Gaily and merrily
You were,
My dear goldfish.

Why then are you so still today,
Not in motion at all?
What's the matter with you?

Maybe you're homesick,
Missing your Mom and Dad,
Your sisters and brothers,
All your dear friends,
Soaked with memories and thoughts of
Your home in the water-land,
Far away, over yonder, of yore.

I do like you so very much.
I do want to live with you,
Forever and ever in this house.
I don't want to lose you.
I don't want to part company from you.
I'll be very sad to be separated from you.
I'll be missing you so very much.
And yet I'll have to set you free.
I must let you go home,
Yes, my dearest goldfish,
In the Han River.
It breaks my heart to see you looking so sad.
It hurts so very much
To keep you away from your folks.
I can't be happy if you are not happy.
I just want you to be happy.
That's all I wish.

Early one fine sunny morning, Mom led me behind a screen where Dad was asleep in the coffin. She said to me in a calm and soft voice, "Tae-Sang, say 'Good Bye' to Dad."

"Daddy—" I barely whispered.

Then Mom held me up tight and walked out of the room. I heard echoes and felt motions of the river flowing in her bosom. I was looking for the passageway to the sea, the peaceful sea of her womb. For the five-year-old child, it was the sea of cosmos where he could play at will to his heart's content, feeling always at home. There, he grew up, becoming a boy and then a young man.

There I swam around, looking for someone like my mother, another 'mom.' There I engaged in philosophy, in search of myself in order to fulfill myself. In so doing, I've come to realize that man was completed in a woman; that loving all women was to love all things in life; that to love was to affirm life itself; and that love was the very source of everything in the world. Having realized this, I composed a poem and dedicated it to her.

Wasn't love the essence of life, indeed?!
Breaths of life were love.
Wings of life were love.
Dreams of life were love.
Completion of life was love.
Wasn't the beginning and
Ending of life love?!
I'd rather live for a moment in love
Than for million years out of love.
Yes, this would be infinitely more blissful.

Were I to be mad,
I'd get mad in living.
Were I to be mad,
I'd get mad in loving.

Were I to be drunk,
I'd get drunk in life.
Were I to be drunk,
I'd get drunk in love.
Really, madly, drunkenly
To death!

Mother...to her, all children were flowers, stars, and rainbows. To her, children were heaven and earth, everything in nature. Spring, summer, autumn, and winter, they were children to her. Yesterday, today, and tomorrow, they were children to her. Hope and despair, dream and reality, young and old, were all the same children to her. So were prince and pauper, princess and harlot, angel and demon, cross and wooden fish, teacher and pupil, master and servant, man and woman, light and shadow, saint and sinner. All her children were one and the same. That child was me. I was everything to her. And she was everything to me. As I was her God, she was my Goddess.

I constantly sang my song of love for her, my first lady. She was the object I ought to worship, for my heart was always pining for her. Or rather, she was COSMOS that turned galaxies, repeating creation and destruction and she was the original element of life.

"Mother, my mother, I love you."

Mother was another word for existence. To her, I couldn't utter the word 'love' carelessly. She was the embodiment of love, from whom I learned about pure love. Although it came through flesh, it came to fruition in spirit, the origin of all beings. She was my heavenly father as well as my earthly mother at the same time. I kept calling her in my heart. As the sound of 'Mother' emanated from my body, it became my life energy. Just like the sea remembered all the winds and waves, just like the sky remembered all the twinkling stars, love made all the rainbows.

"Mother—"

I called her silently. The world was created, maybe, because God, or rather Goddess, needed the objects to love.

Love was she. She and love were synonyms. All things must have been possible because of her.

If heaven was hers, hell too was hers. For as heaven is love, hell is another word for love.

Mother, She is the Light.

Chapter IV

The Second Lady, Athena
She, the Goddess, Seeks Cosmos in Chaos

That day, I was a thirteen-year-old boy. I was fully engaged in the fun-filled plays of children of that age, enjoying the early summer time. All of a sudden, the grown-ups were in a panic, anxious to leave the capital city of Seoul in a hurry. Suddenly all things seemed to have stopped. They didn't know what to do.

"War broke out!" my two-year-older sister Tae-Soon told me, nonchalantly. That day was June 25, 1950. I didn't quite understand what it meant, and yet the word 'war' was familiar to me, as I had been playing war games with my friends. War was a catastrophe for everybody. But to me, it was exciting and thrilling. Truth to tell, for those who would bear it all, all could be blessings.

Early in the summer of the year when I was a seventh grader, the war broke out. Within three days Seoul fell. Like almost everyone else living in Seoul, my family couldn't flee the capital city because the bridges over the Han River were destroyed.

One day, despite my mother's urging that I should not go out, I left my home to see the city streets engulfed in flames following heavy artillery fire and bombings. Debris was everywhere. Walking along the streets, I stopped at the side of a collapsed building. In the middle of an untended garden overgrown with weeds, I discovered some flowers. They were cosmos in pink and red. I gasped with surprise at the cosmos blooming in the hot summer weather. I was used to seeing the cosmos in the fall.

And then, out of the blue, there was a hailstorm. The hail ricocheted off a nearby wall, raising a cloud of dust on the ground. I instinctively crouched down. I soon realized the hail was machine-gun bullets from fighter jets flying low just above the buildings. Moments later I raised my head. When I stood up, I saw bullet holes on the wall and looked at the pink cosmos in the grass. Had I not lain flat on the ground, I would have been hit by bullets.

I scoured the razed city streets, scampering around like a squirrel. According to my friends, the orchards on the outskirts of the city were covered with fruit, and I found some, put them in a bag, and dashed home.

When I was near home, I encountered North Korean soldiers. Fear made me freeze and I stopped dead in my tracks. One of them beckoned me over with a wave. I wanted to run away but my legs wouldn't move.

"What's in the bag?" the soldier asked.

"F…fruits…"

"Where did you get them?"

"G…G…Grandpa gave me."

"Fruits, did you say?"

I felt my death was sure, and the fruits would be taken away for certain. I was on the verge of tears.

"Can you sell the fruits or exchange them for rice?" The soldier lifted a bag of rice to show to me.

"All…alright. I can bring the home-baked bread if you like," I said, much relieved. I knew my mother often baked bread.

"This little comrade is a fine figure of a boy! Okay, if you bring enough bread for all of us, I'll give you two bagsful of rice."

The soldier smiled at me and I smiled back. When I returned with bread, I was welcomed by the soldiers and rewarded with more rice. I befriended the troops and acquired provisions for my family to tide over the hard times. Eventually the North Korean forces retreated from Seoul, and South Korean and American forces re-entered the capital city. I continued my business of hawking whatever I could find to sell. Meanwhile, winter withered all the cosmos.

"The North Koreans are coming back, they say, and the Red Chinese Army too. We have to leave."

My words were uttered in gasps while my mother was busy packing. "Mother, you go ahead of me. I'll follow you."

"What are you talking about? You could be hurt."

Nevertheless, I persisted and stayed behind.

The North Korean and Red Chinese forces came. This time, they couldn't afford to buy anything from me. I walked all the way to the city of Daejon, nearly 100 miles away from Seoul in the central part of the country and joined my family. Everybody was without food, and my family was no better off.

I went hawking in the streets crowded with refugees. I started selling kimpab (sushi) that my mother made. It wasn't anything special, but I had no problem feeding the hungry refugees. I then sold rice-candies in the waiting area and plaza of the railway station. Becoming a bit more venturesome, I jumped over the fence and sold candies at the platform and in the train cars. A steward spotted me and chased after me, shouting, "How you dare come on the train…"

When I jumped off the train, the steward raced after me. The train started moving slowly. I had no choice but to scurry between moving wheels, throwing myself across the rails. Luckily, I didn't get hurt and I managed to lose my pursuer.

Because of the chaos that followed, I didn't have spare clothes and wore my school uniform and cap with my school badge. A man in military uniform stopped to ask me, "Do you go to Kyungbock Middle School?" He was a second lieutenant of the South Korean Army.

"Yes," I replied.

"Do you know Kim Young-chol?"

"Oh, Young-chol, you mean? He's a classmate of mine."

"Really? Young-chol is my younger brother."

"Is that right? My name is Tae-Sang."

"I'm glad to meet you, my little friend."

The officer paused for a moment, then said, "Can you wrap up everything?"

"Do you mean all of these rice-candies?"

"Yes, all of them."

31

After paying me, the second lieutenant bade farewell, patting me on the head. Another time, a female military nursing officer walked towards me and then halted.

"You're having a hard time, aren't you?" she said. I blushed with embarrassment. People kept making eyes at this attractive woman in uniform.

She was beautiful. I just smiled vaguely. Then she handed a large sum of money to me. My initial reaction was to decline to accept the money.

"It's all right. You can keep the money."

She put the money in my pocket. In return for her generous gift of money, I wrapped up everything I had and gave it to her. But my offer was waved aside.

"Now, take care and goodbye!"

The nursing officer hurried away before I could do anything. Stunned, I stared blankly into space with a faraway look, not knowing whither she was gone.

It was in the middle of that winter of 1950 when my mother and I bought many sacks of rice and climbed aboard a freight train. We had heard the price of rice was much higher in the south, where it was swarming with refugees. The freight train moved slowly. Though frozen and tired, we endured the weeklong ordeal perched on a mound of rice sacks, braving the elements.

We got off at the southern town of Gupo, in the South Kyungsang Province, and loaded an ox-cart. When we called on a rice merchant, he complimented me on my enterprise and paid a good price for the load. We made a handsome profit.

We were relieved. Even in the midst of a war, flowers were blooming. The North Korean soldiers who bought my wares, the South Korean soldiers who gave me part of their daily rations, the brother of my classmate who paid for all of my rice-candies, the nursing officer who handed me a good amount of money and the grandfatherly owner of a grain-store who took over the ox-cartload of rice from us, their humanity blossomed in my heart.

I set up a small business in earnest in a flea market of the city, displaying over 100 black market items sold by American GIs trafficking in U.S. Army PX goods. I called aloud for attention to my goodies. One day, I went to the area where the U.S. I Corps was stationed in order to replenish my stock of Yankee goods. When I got there, military equipment and personnel were being loaded onto trucks. The whole unit of troops was moving. I approached the officer sitting in a jeep at the head of a long line of vehicles. Since my English was limited, I managed to utter just a few words, "I your houseboy. Okay?"

The officer looked at me intently and then motioned me to hop onto the back seat of his jeep.

I said breathlessly, "Wait a moment, I must go and speak to Mother."

Smiling, the officer, with his big hands, lifted me and sat me in his front seat, saying something to his driver.

"Yes, sir."

"Where's your mother?"

I directed the driver, pointing towards the market. I told my mother that I was going away with American troops.

From then on, I was a diligent worker, shining shoes, making beds and running errands for officers and the rank and file. Though I was a child, I did not have to be told what to do. Officers and enlisted men showered me with chewing gum, candies, cookies, and chocolate. I took them to my mother whenever I visited her.

U.S. Army I Corps moved north beyond the 38th Parallel and then retreated back south to Seoul. When I finished my job early in the morning, I went to a school set up temporarily for the refugee children in Seoul. The commanding officer who took me as his houseboy was a colonel who loved classical music. Soon, I became a little classical music buff, too.

"If you'd like to study music, I'll send you to the Juilliard School in New York," the officer promised. The commanding officer's tour of Korea would soon be over and he'd be returning to America. One evening the officer wanted to have a word with me.

"I'll be returning home soon," he told me. "You know I've been treating you like my own son. If you decide to come with me to America, I'll adopt you and send you to an American school. What do you think about that?"

"Thank you, sir. But I have to ask my mother."

"Where is she now?"

"She's still in Daejon City."

"All right, then, go talk to your mom."

The next day I went to see her. As always, my mother was very happy to see me. I could not sleep and was not able to tell my mother that an American officer wanted to take me to America and adopt me.

On my return, I said, "I'm sorry. Mother doesn't want me to go to America."

The officer dialed up the phone and talked to someone. After he hung up, he kissed me on my forehead and said, "I understand. Stay well in Korea."

On the morning of the day the officer was leaving for America, an American GI driver came to pick me up and take me somewhere. The officer put his hands on my shoulders and said, "I've asked a good friend of mine to take good care of you. Goodbye, my boy."

The officer was in tears, but I did not cry. I did not want to show a sign of weakness.

Driven away on a jeep, I looked back. The officer was waving to me. When I looked back again, the officer had disappeared from sight. Then, and only then did I burst into tears. Much to my surprise, I was taken to Daejon City.

The commanding officer's friend was also a colonel in charge of the CAC, a United Nations organization for the reconstruction and rehabilitation of war-torn South Korea. Except for the colonel, all the other staff members were civilians representing the United Nations member countries participating in the Korean War. Their living quarters were located in the western suburb of the city. The colonel had a houseboy, but it just so happened that the houseboy of the deputy head of the organization stole something and ran away a couple of days before, so I was assigned to the deputy as a replacement. Thanks to the deputy's kindness and considerations, I could attend another refugee-school in Daejon while working as a houseboy.

The deputy was a retired British colonel and a veteran of both World War I and II. He had a Japanese bayonet scar on his leg and a bullet in his body. After he was discharged from the army following his injury, he served as the governor of a province of New Zealand. The deputy also loved me dearly. He enjoyed having me giving a speech standing on a table in the American military officer's club.

He would say to me, "When I return to England, you come with me. I'll send you to Oxford University, if you want."

While I was working as a houseboy, I met another houseboy who was well informed and a gifted speaker. I couldn't conceal my envy of my friend. I asked my friend's advice.

Surprisingly, my friend's advice was unexpected. "I have a good idea for you. Why don't you go to church?"

"Church?"

"Yeah. All the church-goers are good at speaking, especially the revivalist preachers."

I hesitated before following my friend to a revival service.

Whether due to my acute sensibilities at that early age or my impulsive temperament and tendency to fall head over heels in love with anybody and anything, I became a fanatical believer in Jesus the moment I entered a church. The revivalist speakers emphasized that for one's body to live, one has to breathe, eat, and exercise; for one's soul to be alive, one has to pray, live on the words of the Bible, and evangelize. So I strove to practice, literally, what was preached. Almost every night I went to a revival meeting. I would pray all night long, fast, hand out leaflets of gospel on the streets and in school, totally absorbed in praying, bible reading, and hymn singing. In so doing, I missed out all the fun and frivolous pleasures of adolescence.

As it happened, one day, the retired British colonel collapsed, probably because of his chain-smoking and heavy drinking. He died of cancer six months before his scheduled return to England. I didn't cry, but once more I felt I had been abandoned.

All the fleeting moments became the sweeter and more poignant as time passed, and I became a young man, musing about life.

If a dewdrop is evanescent,
So is life.
Must it be as evanescent
As the bloom of flowers and
The fragrance they exhale!

Must it be a dream,
Must it be a dream,
Life must be a dream,
Must it be dreaming in a dream.

If life is a dream,
Let it be a dream of
Engraving our loving hearts.

Let life be a dream.
If it's not a dream,
How could one bear
The pain and sorrow of
Deer being torn by beasts?

Must it be a breath,
Must it be a breath,
Life must be a breath,
Must it be breathing in a breath.

If life is a breath,
Let it be a breath of
Deer breathing in the sky.

Let life be a breath.
If it's not a breath,
How could one have
All the fun and pleasure of
Deer frolicking,
Braving lightning and thunder?

Let us be deer/dear
The symbol of
Our loving hearts.

Athena, Goddess, She, the Goddess of wisdom, courage, inspiration, civilization, law and justice, strategic warfare, mathematics, strength, strategy, the arts, crafts and skill, is Seeking the Cosmos in the Chaos.

Chapter V

The Third Lady, Truth/Goodness/Beauty
She, the True/Good/Beautiful, Desires the Truth

When I was ten years old, I wrote down a poem, walking on the beach after a thunderstorm:

The Sea

Thou
Symbolizing
Eternity, infinity and the absolute
Art
God.

How
Agonizing
A spectacle is Life in blindness
Tumbled into Thy callous cart
To be such a dreamy sod!

A dreamland of the gull
Of sorrow and loneliness full
Where would it be?
Beyond mortal reach would it be?

May humanity be
A sea of compassion!
My heart itself be
A sea of communion!

I envy Thy heart
Containing
Passions of the sun
And
Fantasies of the sky.

I long for Thy bosom
Nursing
Childlike enthusiasm
And all-embracing mother nature.

Although a drop of water,
It trickles into the sea.

Absurd and wild though it might have been, this poem expressed my instinctive prayer. Undoubtedly, this call of the sea made me seem like a precocious child. But, alas, my desires remained childlike. Preoccupied with self-criticism, I was unable to be as natural or as divine as the sea. Was this fanciful vision a trace of childhood innocence or a vestige of human divinity? I would never know, though I should know as I had suffered so much for it. The words I had used to address myself were now all charged with disparate meanings.

I could feel, welling up within myself, the scene evoking a long and enduring train of reminiscences. For me, I fancied, to love was to be born into cosmos. But alas, much too much to my chagrin, I couldn't love myself.

Wasn't I hopelessly misdirected in the early days of my life when I was going to enlarge my life by emptying all the small things I belittled but of which life was composed?

Perhaps, though, I did not fail in perseverance of striving to live up to my (pen) name Hae-Sim '해심' (in Korean), and '海心' (in Chinese characters), meaning the 'Heart of the Sea.' In this light, maybe, I could stop loathing myself and start loving myself for being a wanderer, as a wise old Korean saying noted, "to perceive the whole of the universe through a blade of grass." Perhaps, then, my sufferings were not in vain after all. Unwittingly, I had come to discover my own unique identity I so anxiously longed to bring to light; not to find shame, but to cherish and to nourish.

From this fountainhead would spring my sense of decency and dignity I so despaired of ever feeling. From this wellspring would begin a pilgrimage of a little drop (be it a dewdrop or a raindrop) trickling into the sea of cosmos, with a few grains of sand or stars serving as my companions on the journey.

"Amongst all the religions of the world, Christianity is the only true religion and the others are all superstitions," the most senior professor of Religious Studies began his lecture with this statement. I was confused. Weren't all religions concerned with believing in and worshiping a superhuman, controlling power or powers, providing standards of morality and achieving true happiness? Making such a statement to his students showed the professor to be completely irresponsible.

When I entered college, I tried to decide on my subject major. College education would civilize me. I would become a 'cultured' person. I expected nothing more. But I first needed to find a map and a compass, for they were indispensable for the voyage. If life was really like a floating 'leaf-boat,' and if I'd like to sail as I wished, I would need to have a sense of direction, above all, a philosophy of life. That's why I chose philosophy and religion as my major subjects.

The professor continued the lecture. "Out of all the denominations, only the Methodists are orthodox, and all the others are heretic... If there are one thousand Christians, only one of them is a true believer..."

I stood up in protest, "Professor, please permit me to ask you a question. If one's faith is precious, wouldn't it be the same with others too?"

"What? What do you dare to mean by that?" The professor was clearly angry.

I lowered my voice, "Professor, I know well-behaved children do not answer back when scolded. However, I am just pointing up the necessity for caution and fair-mindedness, if I may. Listening to your self-righteous statements, I'm reminded of Mahatma Gandhi's remark that, but for Christians, we could all be Christians. If there were no Christianity, there would be no Crusade, Prof—"

Becoming impatient and growing more furious, the Professor yelled, "Go away, you Satan!"

I left the classroom without saying another word, realizing that all attempts at counterargument would be futile.

In high school I had been a fanatical churchgoer. For fear that my soul would be condemned to burn in hell for all eternity, I didn't go near a movie theater. But disappointed with the Church altogether, filled with an infinite curiosity, I determined to explore life itself.

I started voraciously reading previously forbidden novels and watching forbidden movies. However, I was not satisfied with a vicarious thrill of the experience of others in a world of make-believe and fiction. I wanted to have the first-hand experience of characters in all the dramas. I desired to create the 'true-stories' of my own life. From then on, I searched in deadly earnest for the love of my life. I thought it would be nice to find a girl well brought up and take good care of her. It would be nicer if I could meet somebody who had a hard life and make her happier. I even ventured into brothels and rescued some of the young sex slaves by paying off their debts. In so doing, my heart was broken repeatedly.

Then I happened to read a short story that captured my imagination. It was a story of an American soldier serving overseas. One day the soldier entered the military library where he found a copy of Somerset Maugham's 'Of Human Bondage' among books donated by civilians back home.

As he was reading, the soldier was distracted by some interesting musings scribbled on the margin in a feminine hand that aroused his curiosity. He tried to find the writer and, after a long search, he obtained her name and address. Eventually they became pen pals.

When World War Two ended, the soldier was discharged. He and his pen pal arranged to meet at a train station platform. Since each did not know what the other person looked like, he was carrying a copy of the novel and she was wearing a flower in her lapel, just as they told each other. He found someone with a flower in her lapel. It turned out she was an elderly woman. For a second, he was disappointed, and yet he greeted her, introducing himself with a big smile. Without pausing for breath, the old lady whispered something in his ear that sent him flying towards the beautiful young lady who was waiting for him at a nearby restaurant.

This story inspired me to find an ideal life-mate. One such means would be a pen pal. In communicating by letter I was less likely to pre-characterize someone. By exchanging thoughts and feelings, I could get to someone in a relaxed nonjudgmental fashion, I thought.

After leaving the college lecture hall, I abandoned the hereafter and God-oriented religion. I was filled with a longing for someone as yet unknown.

I always had an image of the perfect woman:

There is a Lady Sweet and Kind

There is a lady sweet and kind,
Was never a face so pleased my mind;
I did but see her passing by,
And yet I love her till I die.
           — English poet Barnabe Googe (1540–1594)

I kept on reciting to myself what the masterful Persian poet Halal ud-din Rumi (1207–73) wrote:

I would love to kiss you
(The price of kissing is my life)
Now my loving is running toward my life
Shouting: "What a bargain,
Let's buy it!"

Chapter VI

The Fourth Lady, Cosmos
She, the Cosmos, Is the Taste of Heaven

When I was fourteen years old, I left home and went on a journey. People said I became a vagabond at an early age. One summer night, l wrote a poem:

Cosmos

When I was a boy,
I liked the cosmos
Cozy and coy
Without rhyme or reason to toss.
Later on as a young man
I fell in love with cosmos
Conscious of the significance
Of this flower for me sure,
The symbol of a girl's love pure.
As I cut my wisdom teeth,
I took the cosmopolitan road
Traveling the world far and near
In my pursuit of Cosmos in a chaotic world.
Upon looking back one day,

Forever longing, forever young,
Never aging and never exhausted
By yearning for cosmos,
I'd found unawares numerous cosmos
That had blossomed all along the road
That I had walked.
A dreamland of the bluebird
Looking for a rainbow,
Where could it be?
Over and beyond the stormy clouds,
That's where it could be,
Right there arainbow!

Come autumn, wherever you go in the countryside of Korea, the pure and pretty cosmos, shyly swaying in the breeze, catches the wanderer's eye all along the journey. At times like this, you suffer from an old heartache. As a constant stream of humanity flowed by, I became a young man.

One day in a bakery café in Seoul, Korea, I was instantly captivated by a girl so pure and pretty. It was 'love at first sight.' If she were a flower, what flower would she be? There was a saying that among all the creations of God, the cosmos was the first and the chrysanthemum was the last. While I was in a daze, she was leaving. I hesitated before following her.

She became aware of being followed from downtown Jongno to Sinchon on the outskirts of town.

"Do you have any business with me?" she asked. She had a clear voice.

"Please let me introduce myself. I'm a new philosophy-religion graduate of Seoul National University. I want to make your acquaintance, if I may. Do you mind?"

She blushed scarlet. I was delighted and decided to call her my Cosmos.

I started dating my Cosmos. We frequented music cafes like *C'est Si Bon* and *The Milky Way*, in downtown Seoul. One day we went to see a film, *The Brothers Karamazov*. Waiting in the second-floor lobby for the next show time, she asked, "Do you want to go to the bathroom?"

I didn't feel like going, but I went anyway. The entrances to the men's and women's bathrooms were side by side. I stood for a moment in front of the urinal and a thought crossed my mind that I and my Cosmos were not far apart with only a wall between us. I realized if the distance were shortened by just a few feet, I could be in her.

At the very moment I experienced the contraction of the space. Thereafter, I never felt lonesome again. Anytime, anywhere, I could feel close to anybody. If the whole universe were compressed into a single dot, one could be united with all.

In the meanwhile, a powerful opposition politician asked me to become his secretary. My involvement with the student movement opposing the corrupt and dictatorial government must have caught his attention. I declined the offer because I had other plans. In the future, be it politics, economics or culture, in all walks of life, I thought, it was going to be global, and therefore learning foreign languages was essential. Since middle and high school, I'd been learning English, Japanese, Chinese, German, French, and Spanish. And in college I studied Latin, Greek, Hebrew,

Russian, and Arabic. I became fluent enough in English, German, French, and Spanish to tutor fellow students, businessmen, and military generals.

Being a greenhorn at that age, I decided three jobs were unworthy of a man: secretary, spokesperson, and ghostwriter. If you possessed a modicum of self-respect, I reasoned, why should you run errands, speak for another, or write for somebody? If you could become a secretary, why not become a presidential secretary? Even that was not because I coveted the position of a presidential aide. There's an old saying in Korea: "You've got to enter a tiger's den if you want to catch a tiger." This was not to say I thought of harming anyone, but it was rumored that President Syngman Rhee, the first president of the Republic of (South) Korea, was surrounded by a pack of sycophants and schemers blinding him to the true state of affairs. If I worked for him, I would open up the President's eyes and ears to people's needs and problems. In fact, I had secured glowing recommendations from several VIPs for a protocol post of the Kyungmudae, the President's office—now called the Blue House.

After graduating from the Kyungnam Girl's High School in Busan, my Cosmos attended the School of Pharmacy, Ewha Women's University in Seoul. Before going home for the winter break of 1959, she gave me a copy of Dante's *The Divine Comedy* as a Christmas present. I was going to visit her and meet her parents in Busan as soon as I received my official appointment. In case I couldn't make it for some reason, I also made an appointment to see her on the next Valentine's Day at the Lake Restaurant in Seoul.

A few days later I fled the capital. Because of the active part played in the student movement, I had to go into hiding. After going underground, I wrote a letter to my Cosmos. Writing in ink wouldn't convey the urgency and the intensity of my love for her, so I drew blood from my forearm and calligraphed the note in blood. Apologizing for not keeping the appointment, I begged for understanding and asked her to wait for me until I could contact. My message to her was rolled into a parcel and mailed. Apparently frightened by this shocking 'blood-letter,' she replied with a short note saying, "Please forget me."

Falling into an abyss of despair, I devised a plan on how to take my own life. If I could find a boat, I would row it as far as I could in that great expanse, the sea and the sky, often likened to a life-journey itself. If not, I would simply jump into the sea and swim as far as I could.

As if drawing a long-kept sword, I wrote a suicide note:

Dear Cosmos,

Call me a crazy, stupid madman, or what you may.

I'm going to jump into the sea, into the bosom of the Cosmos.

After sending this parting note off, I threw myself into the East Sea. Were life and death indeed providential? My one life was miraculously spared, escaping from nine deaths. In the hopeless turmoil, I hurt my back and was hospitalized. After my surgery at the Medical Center in Seoul, the simmering student uprising of April 19, 1960, finally erupted.

Reading newspapers one day, I spotted someone identified as Cosmos on the list of donors helping the victims of the Uprising who were killed or wounded by the police. I intuited that it was my Cosmos! She was grieving over my victimhood, for sure. I was deeply moved. Even if I were to breathe my last at that very moment, I could not have been happier. After one surgery, I recuperated but I pretended otherwise and underwent two more surgeries. Following operations on my spine to remove herniated discs, I wished I would have never have awakened from the anesthetic. But even if I came to myself, I would be happy with the vivid memories of my Cosmos forever.

Hospitalized for almost a year, thinking of my Cosmos, day and night, I happened to read a newspaper article on graduating students of Ewha Women's University. My Cosmos was a senior there. Asked about their personal views on marriage, a few students said they didn't want to get married at all.

One observation in particular was penetrating: "A man's life seems too tough and tragic." These words took away my breath and soul.

"Oh, my goodness, my Cosmos thought I was dead and couldn't forget me. And she wouldn't marry. What a horrible thing I've done to her. I've got to set her free from this nonsense."

Then I panicked when I recalled hearing that someone had become impotent after a spinal surgery.

"Have I become impotent too? Even if not, could I father a child?" I asked myself.

I was apprehensive of my conditions. Only after my sperm was tested and I received a clean bill of health, did I write to my Cosmos for an appointment to meet her at the Lake Restaurant on the next Valentine's Day, February 14, 1961. I planned to get the two families together to arrange for the two young people's engagement.

I went to her school to check if she got my letter. The letter was still in the school mailbox, uncollected. I inquired her whereabouts and went to deliver it myself. In no time, after speaking with her, it dawned on me that mine was the typical case of "a misconception at liberty and of a delusion at sea."

She told me that she was seeing another man. Thunderstruck by the harshness of reality, I wished her all the happiness. And I mused.

Was the grass wet with early morning dew to pay my dues of life and love?
Were they dewdrops of life giving and love making, or rather teardrops of joy and sorrow?
Was that for breathing in this magic world to the full, and breathing out to the last
Before transforming back into the mystical essence of the cosmos?

Chapter VII

The Fifth Lady, Chaos

She, the Chaos, Is the Taste of Hell

I was depressed and confused. I understood that one had to see things with the clear eye of a child who could not differentiate good from bad, clean from dirty, true from false, and fearless from fearful. Only then could one share the love that transcended the joys and sorrows of meeting and parting, the love that transcended the distance between time and space. And then one could realize the justification for the existence of everything in the world.

Dewdrops sipped by a cicada become songs; sipped by a bee they become honey; whereas the same dewdrops become poison when imbibed by a snake. But one must not forget that even the venom of a snake could serve a purpose, I reminded myself. The grown-up's greatest trouble was the loss of a child's eye.

I was sick at heart, missing my Cosmos, and mused: 'Though there's no telling whose providence it was for us, you and me, to meet and part, wouldn't it be like the blink of our eyes—like the twinkle of stars? Though there's no telling why the snow and rainstorm come and go in and out of season, don't the dewdrops form at night on a blade of grass and vanish at sunrise as night melts into day like a mirage? Though there's no telling what we're made of, aren't we all drops of life giving and love making that trickle into the sea of cosmos?'

When I was serving in the army, a fellow soldier received a weekly school paper sent by his girlfriend who attended the Ewha Women's University in Seoul. One day an article in the paper caught my fancy. The subject of the article was 'Letter' shared by a professor and a student. The gist of what the professor wrote was that he used to send and receive 'romantic' letters in his younger days, but nowadays his correspondence was all business. The professor added that, no matter how brief it was, what you wrote revealed your soul.

The student's letter was the more challenging one.

"We tend to lie more in correspondence than in conversation," she wrote. "Perhaps," she posited, "it was our common instinctive attempt to camouflage our shortcomings and human weaknesses; to embellish our achievements; to downplay our failures." She ended by saying, "You'd think about the person who wrote or to whom you were writing, at least while reading or writing the letter."

I judged her to be a modest, self-respecting person with a candid mind. "This is the very cosmopolitan girl I've been looking for!" I decided.

I started writing my love letters addressed to her at school. To make sure my letters would be delivered promptly, they were sent by registered express mail. I not only sent letters but also my favorite Korean and foreign verses engraved on wood.

One was Yun Dong-Ju's 'Prologue' from *Sky, Wind, Stars, and Poems* that was posthumously published. Yun Dong-Ju (1917–45) was the most celebrated Korean poet. He died in a Japanese prison six months before World War II came to an end, as South African black activist Steve Biko (1946–77) died in police custody as a result of beatings received.

Yun Dong-Ju's 'Prologue'

Until the day I die, pray,
Not a speck to be ashamed of
Against the sky,
I suffered even for the leaves
Gently swaying in the breeze.
I've got to love all mortals.
And I must walk along the path
Made for me.
Tonight, as always, the stars are grazed
By the wind.

Another was a poem by William Blake (1757–1827):

To see a World in a Grain of Sand
And a Heaven in a Wild Flower.
Hold Infinity in the palm of your hand
And Eternity in an hour.

All were sent, together with records of Ludwig van Beethoven's symphonies, "Die Winterreise," a song cycle of Franz Schubert, consisting of 24 songs set to poems of

Wilhelm Muller, "The Magic Flute (Die Zauberflöte)," an opera by Wolfgang Amadeus Mozart, and a collection of Negro spirituals. Just in case she didn't have a record player, I even sent a portable one. Though I received no reply, I was confident she was getting her mail since there had been none marked "return to sender." So I kept on untiringly.

After six months, I got a reply to my daily correspondence. Her home address was on the envelope. This was enough encouragement, and on a weekend pass to leave my military base, I was going to visit the girl I had been dreaming about night and day. My pulse fluttered and my stomach was full of butterflies.

The instant I saw the girl in person, I could hardly breathe. The ecstasy of our first meeting was really beyond description. Her father, a celebrated poet, was kidnapped by the North during the Korean War. She was living with her novelist mother and a younger sister in a picture-perfect house in the suburbs.

She was excited, too. While receiving the mail from me, she'd written a short story entitled Man in Blue Uniform, using me as the major character, and she'd just been notified by post that her story was a winner in a literary contest.

"When I receive the prize money," she said, "I will send you a gift subscription to *Ssassanggye* (meaning World of Thoughts)." This then very popular highbrow monthly magazine was later forced to cease publication by the military government (right after I was offered the editorship by the publisher).

A few days after her notice of winning, I went to the award ceremony to congratulate her on making her debut as a writer, carrying a gift set of fountain pens. For some reason, she didn't show up and I picked up the prize on her behalf and took it to her home. She was out, and I left the gift of pens with her mother.

When I left her home to return to my base after visiting her for the third time, it began to rain. Before we left for the bus stop, she picked two cherries from her garden and handed them to me. She seemed unaware of what she had done. Holding the two cherries in my hand, I thrilled at the symbolism. The early summer rain soaked through the tear in the umbrella, quickening our pulses and warming our breaths. Seeing me off at the bus stop, she agreed to another date the following weekend.

When I took the last bus to my base the night of the third date, all the passengers were KATUSA (Korean Augmentation to the U.S. Army stationed in Korea) except one lone GI. Many were clearly drunk.

"That Yankee is all by himself, isn't he? I feel lousy. Shall we beat him up?"

"Oh yeah, why not?"

"Yeah, yeah, all Yanks are SOBs. Why don't we tell them to leave us alone and just go back to their own country?"

They were calling the quietly sitting GI names in Korean, even though they could speak English.

"Let's stop this, for goodness' sake. It's such a cowardly attack on a helpless guy!" I protested.

Though hearing these admonishing words, the noisy crowd failed to quiet down.

"What? Cowardly? Don't you dare say that again."

Following a momentary silence, someone spat.

"Aren't we all members of KATUSA defending our country with the help of the U.S. Army?" I gently reminded my fellow soldier passengers.

Then someone else yelled, "Hey, driver, stop the bus!"

When the driver pulled over, a mob of KATUSA members dragged me out of the bus and bombarded me with kicks and punches. When I opened my eyes, I was in a military hospital, enveloped in bandages.

My face was swollen from beatings, yet I didn't feel myself aggrieved. Instead I commiserated with the attackers. I was aware, only too well, of how we were being treated by our American comrades-in-arms. We were constantly subject to ridicule and humiliation. So I understood that I was an easy prey for them to vent their pent-up rage and frustration.

In February 1961, I enlisted with the Republic of (South) Korean Army, despite the fact that I was exempted from conscription (military service) on the medical grounds of my physical condition. Had I been happily reunited and engaged in love with my Cosmos, I had planned to prepare for the state exam to become a diplomat, someone like Dag Hammarskjold, a Swedish diplomat who served as the second Secretary-General of the United Nations from April 1953 until his death in a plane crash in September 1961. For this purpose, I had rented a room at a Buddhist temple in the Sorak Mountain near the east coast where I had earlier attempted a suicide.

On completing basic and adjunctive training, I was posted to the Aviation Wing of the Capital Division, which later fought in the Vietnam War. Because of my spinal surgery, I had to wear a corset and was excused from strenuous physical exercises. Allowed just to sit and watch, I was nicknamed 'The Head Monk of Hae-In-Sa,' a well-known Buddhist temple in Korea.

Stationed at a military airstrip that was busy with helicopters and reconnaissance planes taking off and landing, I served as an interpreter for Korean and American pilots and other officers. One day I caught the attention of the commanding general of the 8th U.S. Army and was transferred to KATUSA. I was assigned to the U.S. Army Chemical Depot and the U.S. Army 547 Engineer Corps stationed in Buchon County, Gyungghee Province, near Kimpo Airport. There were hundreds of KATUSA members and scores of Korean civilian employees, besides U.S. Army personnel, at the base.

Under the chain of command headed by a ROK, Republic of (South) Korea Army Major and followed by officers of junior rank, sergeants 1st class, staff sergeants and sergeants, KATUSA members were doing all sorts of menial tasks—from cleaning mess halls and utensils, grass-cutting, snow-shoveling, loading and unloading, to repairing roads—almost like slaves. We were often insulted as 'slicky boys,' meaning petty thieves, by the American GIs. Even so, the ROK Army soldiers were eager to become KATUSA members for the comfort of better facilities and provisions at the U.S. Army bases.

I, too, was incensed by the insulting remarks. They enraged me by their deliberate and continual injustice. But I couldn't blame the Americans. Koreans were, in part, responsible for the ill treatment, I thought. I decided to write an open letter to my fellow KATUSA members, reminding them that one has to behave like a decent human being in order to be treated like one: "Let's become excellent emissaries representing Korean people."

I instantly became a troublemaker to those in charge of KATUSA personnel. Those in charge were, in fact, responsible for all the corrupt and shameless practices going on that brought all the disgrace and dishonor to all the Korean people and KATUSA members. I received several threatening warnings. One was, "If you want to save your life, go back to the ROK Army." Becoming a fugitive was out of question.

One evening, a gang of former street bullies and martial arts experts dragged me to a little valley some distance away. I did not forget an old saying, "If you don't lose your head and heart, you can survive a tiger's attack."

I was always more spirited whenever I was challenged. Years before, it was a sports day at my grade school. I was the runner in the last leg of a relay race. One foot was badly cut by a broken piece of glass during a soccer match earlier in the day and had been wrapped, yet I ran faster than usual to victory with a long trail of bandage soaked in blood, prompting a thunderous applause.

Even though I exercised on parallel and high bars in grade school, practiced judo in middle and high school and Taekwondo (Korean martial arts) in college, I was no match for the villains armed with baseball bats, metal bars, and knives. I used to engage black-belt-holders and was, more often than not, victorious, but obstinately refused to be graded and wear belts in any color. It was my credo to go against the grain, believing "no technique is the best technique."

Surrounded by more than ten guys at the sunset in the valley, still, I could see each of them as a big softie, or a timorous soul, not a real tough guy. I'd been observing closely that in movies, as well as in the real-life events, the outcome was decided well before the fight even began, be it a debate, a fistfight, a sword fight or a gunfight. Whoever cowered first became the vanquished.

I, though smaller in size, must have had more guts to overpower my opponents. After disengaging myself from those poor guys thrown into disarray, frightened out of their senses, I returned to the base and held a ballot of KATUSA members. If the majority cast a vote of 'no confidence' in me, I proposed to return to the ROK Army voluntarily. The vote was unanimous with a few abstentions, pleading me not to go and urging me on as I cleaned up the mess. Only the officers in charge left, as the official order for the return of all the non-commissioned officers was revoked at the last minute at my request. In those days, KATUSA members dreaded being sent back to the ROK Army. In their place, I was given overall responsibilities for KATUSA personnel as a Non-Commissioned-Officer-In-Charge with a double promotion of rank from private first class to sergeant.

After improving the moral fiber of KATUSA personnel, I had to fight hard for equal rights. In an effort to reason with the overbearing GIs, I wrote another open letter, this time in English, to all the U.S. military officers and enlisted men stationed in Korea. I called their attention to the fact that no matter how deeply grateful Korean people in the South were to U.S. Forces fighting against Communist North Korea, the American military had come to Korea, first and foremost, for the interest of the U.S.A. They wanted to keep South Korea as their advance stronghold against the Soviet Union in the geopolitics of the world.

"Was it just to play a savior or Santa Claus for charity?" I asked in earnest. Wasn't it much less to colonize Korea in the name of Democracy and Capitalism; still less to incite anti-Americanism by faultfinding and trampling on the human rights and pride of Korean people? I also reminded them of the historic fact that Korea was divided against our own will and wishes at the end of the World War II when Korea was liberated from Japanese occupation by both American and Soviet forces. Hence the Korean War broke out in the heat of Cold War tension between the two super powers.

I wrote, citing a passage or two like, "A great man shows his greatness by the way he treats a little man," and "the manner of giving shows the character of the giver more than the gift itself."

"Let's remember Jesus's words, that man lives not by bread alone," I suggested.

I was fearful that my letter might have repercussions for the whole KATUSA contingent serving with the U.S. Army. The effect of the letter, however, was unexpectedly beneficial to all concerned. I won the official commendation with 'a letter of appreciation' from the commanding officer of the U.S. detachment for raising the morale of KATUSA personnel and making a very positive contribution to the successful close cooperation with the U.S. Forces.

I was happy. Even though I had been hospitalized following the beating by fellow KATUSA members, because of the two cherries I received from my pen pal girlfriend that night, I was euphoric. What does it matter if

I lost a few pennies, now that I owned the most precious treasure of treasures?

Yet again, maybe it wasn't meant to be. 'Ah! Was it you? Though stars were shining in the sky... No matter how hard I tried, my efforts were in vain... I couldn't hold your cold hand and warm it up...' just like operatic lyrics.

I received a 'Dear John' letter from my 'ideal' pen pal girlfriend. It came out of the blue. It happened the very next day, after I told of my major at college and of my younger brother who didn't go to college.

'What do you learn in college?' I had to ask myself. If all that a college education fostered was arrogance and vanity, then I would take it as a consolation that my brother didn't go to such a factory that mass-produced 'human parasites.' I wouldn't recommend a higher education to anybody and I wouldn't marry a college graduate, I swore.

Her mother's viewpoint was easy to understand. Among all the available suitors, why not some with more practical value, such as medicine, law, or economics? Had he gone to a Divinity School, at least he could have become a church minister or a pastor. He wouldn't be able to feed my daughter. She must have been dismayed.

"What school did you go to?" she asked me when I made my first visit.

"I went to the College of Liberal Arts and Sciences, Seoul National University," the most prestigious university in Korea.

With that, she might have expected that I had attended the department of Political Science or English. Asked about my siblings, I told her that a sister was studying abroad. So the assumption that I was from a well-to-do family turned out to be incorrect in the light of the fact that my younger brother never went to college. It was hard for a parent to grasp and accommodate the discrepancy. I understood the reason for the abrupt break-up. It had to do with a child's future security.

Until then, I always withdrew at once whenever my advances to a girl were not welcome, even if not rejected outright. But this time, it didn't seem like my pen pal girlfriend's rejection was due to her own volition at all. I kept on pleading with her by telephone and in writing not to follow anybody's dictates but to follow her own heart and soul. My entreaty was of no avail. I even sought her younger sister's moral support. If one could move heaven and earth, why not another human being?

But the two sisters seemed unable to free themselves from their mother's absolute influence on them. I became desperate and wrote a poem entitled "I accuse the Old Generation of Panderism." I addressed it to the mother and her two daughters and mailed it.

On the day I was discharged from the armed forces, I hurried to my pen pal girlfriend's home. As I rang the doorbell, she peeped over the wall and bolted the gate securely before disappearing into the house. I jumped over the wall, as if to rescue the princess imprisoned in a castle— like Hong Kil-Dong, Korea's most legendary outlaw. I then knocked on the door. Meanwhile, she ran barefoot to fetch her aunt, a neighbor, I discovered later.

What baffled and even angered me was the fact that her mother was a famous writer of distinction, who was supposed to lead the way in love as well as in life. How could such a mentor so cruelly nip young love? I grimly held out hope. From somewhere a thin piece of aurora began spreading across the crumpled drawing paper of my romantic sketchbook.

One day I chanced upon my former pen pal girlfriend and began following her. She was already a young lady, no longer a girlish figure. It was one of those days when I was wandering aimlessly around the streets like a sleepwalker, half-awake from a sweet dream. She entered the building of *The Korea Herald*, an English-language daily published in Seoul. I learned from the front desk guard that she was working in the paper's research department.

Out of military service, I went back to school, attending The Hankuk University of Foreign Studies in Seoul while running a bookstore, The Duk-Hae Book Gallery. The name was a combination of the first letter of my mother's first name, Duk-Soon, and that of my pen name, Hae-Sim, with Duk-Hae 덕해 in Korean alphabet and 德海 in Chinese characters meaning 'The Sea of Virtue.'

One morning I happened to read an article in *The Korea Times*, another English-language daily published in Seoul. It was written by an American wife of a Korean man. She wrote about human relationships, especially between a man and a woman. The article provoked discussion. I wrote to the editor, presenting my own thoughts, which were based on my pen pal experience. Much to my surprise, my article appeared in the same 'Thoughts of The Times' column the next day. I took a copy to show to my former pen pal girlfriend. If it wasn't her own idea to sever our relationship so abruptly, would she reconsider her decision and resume seeing me?

"I'll think about it and let you know shortly," she replied. I didn't hear from her for some time.

Meanwhile, there was an oratorical contest in English for students sponsored by *The Korea Herald*.

"I accuse the old generation of panderism!" I roared.

By sheer coincidence, *The Korea Herald* was currently recruiting new reporters. I finished top in the written exam and interview, and became a reporter.

A few days later, someone wanted to see me. It was a former reporter of *The Korea Herald* who had recently left, joining a new Korean-language daily *The Joongang Ilbo* (The Joongang Daily).

"I understand that you and Miss Kim had a brief acquaintance in the past. I've been dating her for several months and we are going to get married soon. So give her up, if you please," the reporter formally requested.

I felt challenged, "If Miss Kim were a slave or mere chattel, perhaps we could fight a duel to take her," I replied. "But it's up to her, isn't it?"

"If you want to hear what she has to say, I'll arrange a meeting, if I may," the guy said.

"You don't need to do that. I'll find out myself," I responded with a smirk. I went straight to her.

"Didn't you accuse the old generation of panderism?" she asked. "Since you called my mom a 'madam,' you treated me like a prostitute. How could I see a man again who insulted us so cruelly?" Her answer was an unequivocal 'No.'

"I understand. I won't bother you anymore," I replied. "Please accept my sincere apologies. I wish you all the happiness." And then I added, "I just want you to remember that though a dewdrop vanishes without a trace when it evaporates, it was a dewdrop real and true while it was a dewdrop."

"What do you mean by that?" she protested. I gave a wry smile and left.

When I returned home, I recited from Kahlil Gibran's *The Garden of the Prophet*, a lyrical celebration of the mystical beauty of Nature:

"The image of the morning sun in a dewdrop is not less than the sun.
The reflection of life in your soul is not less than life.

The dewdrop mirrors the light because it is one with light, and you reflect life because you and life are one.

When darkness is upon you, say: 'This darkness is dawn not yet born; and though night's travail be full upon me, yet shall dawn be born unto me even as unto the hills.'

The dewdrop rounding its sphere in the dusk of the lily is not unlike yourself gathering your soul in the heart of God.
Shall a dewdrop say: 'But once in a thousand years am I even a dewdrop,' speak you and answer it saying: 'Know you not that the light of all the years is shining in your circle?'"

Then, after handing my resignation to *The Korea Herald,* I joined *The Korea Times* and opened a pub for moonlighting. I named the pub '해심' (in Korean), and

'海心' (in Chinese), meaning 'The Heart of The Sea,' the pen name I gave myself in my childhood. It became very popular with romantics—the students of life and love.

The days passed and I became a middle-aged man. As it happened, twenty-five years later my former pen pal girlfriend and I met again in New York. We were finally united. Yet again, it was brief. Must it be in the bud, as the saying in Latin goes: "Finis Origine Pendet." (The beginning foretells the end.)

Was it happenstance that *Love in the Time of Cholera*, a love story by Gabriel Garcia Marques, was published in the same year? The novel begins with this opening sentence: "IT WAS INEVITABLE."

In their youth, Florentino and Fermina fall passionately in love. When Fermina eventually chooses to marry a wealthy doctor, Florentino is devastated. At first nothing seems inevitable, only an unreciprocated love affair. But his prayers are answered after some fifty years. Was what happened to my former pen pal girlfriend and me inevitable?

I recalled what Frau Eva in Hermann Hesse's *Demian* said:

"You must not give way to desires which you don't believe in… You should, however, either be capable of renouncing these desires or feel wholly justified in having them. Once you are able to make your request in such a way that you will be quite certain of its fulfillment, then the fulfillment will come."

We met again. My former pen pal girlfriend and her younger sister became famous novelists themselves, like their mother. Each of the two sisters was the recipient of the prestigious Lee Sang (a genius poet 1910–37) Literary Prize in Korea. During the ten months of our second marriage for both of us, she wrote her new two-volume novel titled "*Man with Flowers,*" a sort of a sequel to "*Man in Blue Uniform,*" a short story she composed as her debut piece to win a prize a quarter of a century earlier. For both works she used me as the main character. What's more titillating was her serious suggestion of a *menage a trois* with her sister, transcending all the mundane morality and ethical norms. Although I was unable to take it up, I felt immensely grateful to her for the far-out offer.

To be sad, or satisfied, with the truth that you get to keep your child in your arms only until the child leaves the nest may be a choice, not a temperament. I wished her all the happiness once more, for the last time, as she flew away into 'the sky of arts' after taking as much nourishment she needed from 'the nest of life' I provided.

I was happy that I loved her nonetheless. It was the taste of the most exciting and pleasurable 'hell,' all right!

Chapter VIII

The Sixth Lady, United Kingdom
She, the United Kingdom, Is a Strange and Beautiful Land of Goblins

One never knows what's in store. What seemed impossible, like catching a heavenly star, could sometimes happen in the real life.

Whenever I went to Kimpo Airport near Seoul (before Incheon International Airport was built) to welcome or see someone off, those privileged to walk up or down a boarding ramp were aliens from other planets to me. At one time, I was saddened by the news that hundreds of people lost their lives in an airplane crash over the East Sea between Korea and Japan. At the same time, I was even more shocked by a disturbing thought crossing my mind. It was the sense of schadenfreude, a feeling of pleasure at the bad things that happen to other people. For a moment I couldn't help feeling the joy of seeing the fall of the 'high-flyers,' the envy of the 'low-crawlers' and I could commiserate with the country boys throwing rocks at passing trains.

An unexpected opportunity came my way. After working for an American educational publisher as their

Korean representative for two years, I was offered a transfer to Australia. But in those days, the Australian government didn't issue a permanent resident visa to a non-European. I was sent to the United Kingdom, instead.

It took a whole month for my family with three young children, aged three months to three years, to make the journey overseas to London from Seoul. Making the most of this unimaginable chance to travel abroad with our whole family, we had stopovers for sightseeing in Tokyo, Hong Kong, Bangkok, Rome, Athens, Paris, and Amsterdam.

Upon arrival in England, I found the civil, but cool, reception, a mixture of condescension and reserve hard to take. The English 'gentlemen' I had to work with seemed to have a hangover from their memories and sentiments of bygone Pax Britannica days. I was subject to all kinds of subtle, implicit discrimination. I could understand why they must have felt affronted. Why on earth did they have to bring someone from an almost unheard of backward place called Korea, as if there were no competent people in the U.K.?

Determined not to become a laughingstock and sent back, I worked like mad. I traveled throughout Great Britain, including Wales and Scotland, to visit all the universities and colleges. I presented new titles for textbook adoptions and library orders. I represented about 50 American publishers whose publications were distributed all over the world by my employer, an international corporation. Besides holding more than 200 book exhibitions a year, I attended academic conferences for market research. In so doing, I compiled an up-to-date mailing list of faculty members and librarians and contributed to a large increase in sales. I was away from home and with my family briefly on weekends. Even so, I was satisfied with results that made it all worthwhile.

While I was settling in doing 'a great job,' I was offered another transfer, this time to Singapore. But the terms were unacceptable. Relocation costs provided made no allowance for our housing and children's education. Singaporean nationals lived in their government-subsidized, low-cost apartments and their children went to Chinese-speaking local public schools free of charge. I couldn't afford to send my children to an English-speaking international school. The private school fee for one child was more than my annual salary. When I declined the offer of transfer, I was made redundant in my job. Severance pay was only a week's wage for each year I worked in the U.K. They wouldn't pay the moving expenses and airplane tickets for my family to return to Korea. They were not obligated because it was not stipulated in the contract. It was an oversight on my part not to have asked for a revised written contract of employment when I was being transferred from Korea.

Unable to return to Korea or to seek a new employment, prohibited by the work permit my former employer had obtained for me to work in the U.K., my family of five was stranded in a foreign land. I consulted with half a dozen lawyers in London. They told me I had no case legally, though morally I did. In their opinion, my former employer was not at fault. They paid me the severance pay in accordance with the legal requirements.

Surprisingly, a couple of national papers and a local daily reported on the plight of my family, but to no avail. A

Labor Party Member of Parliament representing the district where my family resided wrote a formal letter on my behalf, threatening to raise the issue in the British Parliament. He had a meeting with an executive of my former employer. Still, all the efforts were in vain.

As a last resort I went to the Industrial Tribunal. My former employer was represented by a group of American and British lawyers. Since I had no money to hire a lawyer, and no lawyer offered to represent me, I had to represent myself.

At the end of a yearlong trial came a judgment from the Tribunal. The chairman and his two supporting judges heard the case. It was a unanimous decision that I was unfairly dismissed. Everybody complimented and congratulated me on my victory, even the company's lawyers. The British media reported on my case as a story of "Boy David beating Goliath."

A sure thing in the world. There's all the beauty one cares to behold; all the magic and mystery to wonder, as a child marvels, that stars can exist. From one's birth onward, each breath taken in and out, each moment to live and love, everything is a miracle, be it a blade of grass, a flower, a dewdrop, a raindrop, a snowflake, a ray of moonlight or sunlight, the twinkle of stars, the wind, the sea, the sky, the cosmos. All are more than miracles, infinitely mysterious and sorrowfully and sadly beautiful beyond belief.

Chapter IX

The Seventh Lady, Child
She, the Child, Sings Songs of Cosmic Music

Always changing and impermanent though life is,
Troubled and sorrowful though life is,
What a blessing to be born than not to be born at all!
What felicity to love somebody,
Even if you may be crossed in love and heartbroken!
Aren't all beings born from the Cosmos of Love?!

The years passed and I became an old man. I, and my three grandchildren, Elijah, Theodore, and Julia, we were sitting on the shore, looking up at the sky strewn with stardust.

Gazing at the stars, six-year-old Theodore said, "Why don't you ask me where I come from?"

I responded, "Even when you go back, you'll still be in my heart. So it really doesn't matter whether you leave or stay."

"That's true. Do you still miss your Cosmos?" ten-year-old Elijah asked me.

"Of course, everything is the sea of cosmos for me."

After a bit of silence, I continued, "I've grown old now. I'm at the age to compose a poem eulogizing my own death beforehand."

"What's that?" my three-year-old only granddaughter, Julia, asked with a lovely grimace.

"In actual fact, it's a eulogy to life."

The children became very quiet.

I shed tears, thinking aloud, "How much more precious is a moment of human existence than the eternity of divinity meaningless to mortals!"

Raising my body, I looked at the night sea. There was the sea of cosmos spread out in front of me. I paused for a moment, then went on to elaborate on the 'eulogy to life,' while the three children fell asleep, one by one, in my arms, Julia on my lap and Elijah and Theodore at my sides.

Greek philosopher Epicurus' dictum 'carpe diem' epitomizes his philosophy of life. This two-word phrase literally means 'to seize the day.' It is used to urge someone to make the most of the present time and give little thought to the future, to enjoy the present, as opposed to placing all the hope in the future. It also presents youth as ephemeral and advises the pursuit of pleasure.

"The truth is," I continued, "children are the embodiment of happiness, enjoying life instinctively as the great practitioners of this maxim of Epicurean philosophy. Even their cries are not cries but shrieks of laughter; the cosmic sound of child-song; the ancient music of joy and thankfulness. They are our native symphonic tunes in rhythm with the sea to celebrate our original blessing and our ultimate destination. It's our cosmic chorus:

"Star One, Me One; Star Two, Me Two; Star Three, Me Three… This is the Cosmic Cantata."

The children were fast asleep. There was only the celestial music of all the stars in the wind blowing from the summer sea. Sitting with the children, I saw the stars of the night-sea and had a vision of cosmos flowering everywhere. Looking back on my earlier days, I was amazed at what happened all along. I took a walk down memory lane.

I never married my Cosmos. A bastion of my virginity collapsed unexpectedly. Repulsed by grownup's self-righteous hypocrisy from early on, I posed as a 'lamb in wolf's clothing.' My crude behavior attracted many girls, but despite my vulgar language, I had always acted like a saint until one fateful night.

As if a monkey falls from a tree by an unforeseen accident under the influence of alcohol, I happened to sleep with a girl without having had a date with her. Feeling morally responsible, I proposed to marry her. But this very smart and independent-minded young lady, to my great surprise, rejected me, saying we didn't have to get married just because we'd had sex. Having always believed that 'action speaks louder than words,' I decided to go by her action, not by her words, and tried hard to persuade her to marry me. To make matters worse, her family put up a strong opposition.

Undeterred, and more determined to overcome all adversities, I persevered and two years later we married, but the marriage ended two years after that. Soon after getting a divorce, I learned that she was pregnant with our third child. So I decided to remarry her and to make our marriage work for the sake of the children.

After trying harder for eighteen more years, however, we were divorced for the second time due to our intrinsic and unremitting incompatibility. I learned, the hard way, that you couldn't change yourself, let alone others. A cat is a cat. It cannot become a dog or vice versa, so to speak. That is to say that one has to like it or not 'as is.' Perhaps it was a wrong match from the beginning. Had we truly loved each other, we might have been able to transcend all the differences, difficulties, weaknesses, and misfortunes.

In retrospect, since my early childhood, I had been influenced by sayings of great people. Brainwashed and hypnotized, I would tell myself that mine was a big fire, unlike a candle's flame or small fire easily extinguished even by a breeze. No, mine was more like an eternal star that came to shine as soon as the sky was dark enough, or like a kite that rose highest against the wind, not with it. Thus, I was never discouraged by anything. On the contrary, I was ever more heartened and inspired, come what may.

Striving desperately for over eighty years, I came to realize, at last, that nothing could be forced against the nature of things. Anything that's meant to happen will happen, and if it is not meant to happen, it never will, no matter what.

And yet, it might be possible to mold oneself one way or other, quite early on, in all probability.

Like Hae-a, my oldest child, everybody living on earth must have been protected by one's own guardian angel. Otherwise, how could anyone live through rough times: all the disasters, calamities, and catastrophes? One never knows what to expect from one day to the next, as the landscape, seascape, moonscape, and dreamscape are always changing.

If 'head-works' were thoughts, 'heart-works' might be called arts. From my early childhood, I liked songs and enjoyed music, being sentimental and sensitive to everything, like all children. When I heard a song, the words fascinated me and I was instantly carried away by the melodies. But was I born tone-deaf? I couldn't sing along with the music. Then what made my three children become musicians?

The first thing I did in my married life was to buy a piano, a deluxe stereo system, and hundreds of records in an effort to make it up to my wife. Her family almost disowned her for marrying me, with no prospects or fortune to inherit. She left her piano at her parents' home, a gift on entering a prestigious girls' middle school in Seoul. The audio system and many records she had bought with her own money, earned as a bank employee after college, were also left behind with her parents. Since she didn't continue to play the piano regularly, it was less functional and more decorative. But after our children were born, the piano became a toy again which she could play with them.

To me, who grew up like a street urchin, the Western classical music was something a child born with a silver spoon in one's mouth could indulge in, just like the upstarts who monopolized playing golf in South Korea after the 'Liberation' of Korea from the Japanese at the end of World War II.

When my family moved to England, our children went to a local school in Luton, Bedfordshire. One day, an itinerant music teacher visited the school our oldest child,

Hae-a, attended. Pupils interested in learning to play an instrument were given just a ten-minute lesson a week and instruments were loaned to them by the school. Thus began music lessons for our children, one after another, the oldest and the youngest on the violin and the middle one on the cello.

Before long, a few months after they started making all kinds of noise, we had to leave England for Hawaii, where their grandma and two aunts lived. Short though it was, they must have enjoyed the lessons enough to practice hard and do well. Their music teachers were sad that they had to leave.

Soon after we arrived in Hawaii, I received a letter inviting our children to return. I was deeply grateful to the music teachers who had made arrangements for auditions at the Chetham's School of Music in Manchester, England. No matter how slim a chance it was, I couldn't throw it away. I would rather cast away all the money for the airfares. Although we didn't expect any of our girls to pass the auditions, I was not going to deprive them of a thousandth of a one percent chance of success. Much to everyone's surprise, all three passed and were accepted. But it was a very expensive boarding school, way beyond our means. So there was nothing we could do about it. We were just about to go back to Hawaii when the school offered full scholarships to the three little sisters, a godsend undreamed of.

Thus, it came to pass that the children left home early, at the ages seven to ten. Had music been forced upon them, they would have feigned interest at first but they would have quit too soon. This seemed to be an example of the effect of one's own inclination. If one liked it, whatever it was, one couldn't help doing it with enthusiasm, without even making an effort and it became so much fun.

In the hope that my children would stay young and childlike forever; that they would love everything and not miss a thing, I named them with one common syllable "a" '아' in Korean alphabet, (meaning 'child' in Chinese character '兒') in their first names. Praying they would live on the cosmic energy of the sea, the sky, and the stars, I named them with another Chinese character in each name as Hae-a, 해아, 海兒, meaning the Sea-child; Su-a, 수아,秀兒, meaning the Sky-child (of excellence); and Song-a, 성아, 星兒, meaning the Star-child. Didn't the American Native Indians go into the woods for a revelation as what to name themselves? Long may they continue to live up to their names like a long-lasting couple growing to look alike in time. All children are very dear to their parents, but they are infinitely more endearing and sweeter to their grandparents. Everything they do is so amazingly wonderful and heart-achingly precious, to be cherished for eternity.

My youngest daughter, Song-a, displayed her star quality from her early days. Thank her lucky star for its namesake! She did her impressions of celebrities on T.V. and everybody was captivated by her performance. Even before she went to a nursery school, she would shoo away all the boys flocking around her like a swarm of flies. She would do so without uttering a sound. She just gave them a sharp look or the lyric expressions on the face. She would talk down to grown-ups, using more grownup vocabulary. I couldn't admonish her. Every time I tried to do so, I was instantly disarmed. When I yelled at her in a burst of anger, she put me in my place right off by raising her tiny index finger to her pretty lips or whispering in my ear, "You don't have to shout." And I hushed.

At times she seemed to be a dainty sprite popped out of a myth or a fairy tale. When I appeared to be lecturing her about her homework, she looked me straight in the eye like a child looking at a gorilla behind the bars in a zoo. When I went to the bathroom, she was there right behind me and surprised me peeing. And she asked, "Dad, did you shake?"

My middle one, Su-a, was extraordinary, even as an infant. Was it due to her name? Was she a born rebel? She wouldn't do anything if she were told to do it. If she were told not to do it, she would do it one way or another. Whatever she did, she did as much, and when she wanted. That's why people called her "Crazy Super Su-a". Once her interest was awakened, there was no stopping her. When she laughed, she would roll over and over on the floor. Life was a time for play and the world was her playground. This little playgirl never stopped until she had exhausted herself. No wonder she would often fall asleep at the dinner table. She was a fearless adventurer.

After we arrived in England on February 14, 1972, we lived in a rented house in Kings Langley, Hertfordshire. One Sunday morning I looked into the children's bedroom. The oldest and the youngest were still asleep. But the middle one's bed was empty. I found her downstairs. She was in a complete daze after taking a whole bottle of baby aspirins as if they were candies. Apparently one-and-a-half-year-old Su-a climbed up a high chair at the breakfast table and took the bottle out of a medicine cabinet in the kitchen. She was rushed to the hospital and her life was saved.

That summer we were vacationing in Cornwall in S.W. England. We rented a camper on a hill near the beach. While preparing the breakfast one morning, I looked out the window and saw our car, parked next to the camper, was slowly moving down the hill. Even more shocking was a live daredevil stunt action of two-year-old Su-a jumping out of the driver's seat from the rolling car. What if she had been run over by the car? The car crashed into a ditch at the bottom of the hill. She must have climbed into the car and released the handbrake.

At one time when Su-a was three, I came home at the weekend as usual from my weekly business trip. I had a lot to tell my wife. Su-a kept interrupting us and she got a scolding from her mother for not waiting until we finished talking. Still, she didn't stop and tried to engage me in conversation. Beginning to get annoyed with her persistence, I yelled at her to shut up. She didn't even blink.

"Dad, now you talk to Mom," she replied, with a nonchalant shrug and left the room.

Su-a always had to have the last word in any argument. She was so quick-witted, most often one or two steps ahead of everybody. When we went shopping, not sure what to buy, we usually asked Su-a for a smart choice. Talking to Su-a, I burst out laughing time and again waving an invisible flag of unconditional surrender, for she had already presented a more convincing counter-argument even before I could make out a case.

Soon after her older sister, Hae-a, started on the violin unbeknownst to her parents, Su-a went to Hae-a's violin teacher to ask for a cello teacher, saying she liked the cello sound better. The day she came home with a quarter-size cello loaned to her by the school, she kept scraping away at the cello for six hours, skipping supper altogether.

Later, after taking a couple of lessons, Su-a followed Hae-a to a rehearsal for the Youth Orchestra concert in the evening. The rest of us arrived at the concert hall in good time. Until the concert started, Su-a didn't come to sit with us. I was beginning to feel nervous and distinctly uneasy about Su-a's whereabouts. The moment I looked at the stage, I was frightened out of my wits and almost fainted. Seven-year-old Su-a was playing in the orchestra, sitting on the edge of a chair with her legs dangling over the sides of her tiny cello among much bigger children, including high school students.

I thought it must have been on account of her name. I thought, too, 'long may it continue.'

My firstborn Hae-a, her quiet and calm outward appearance notwithstanding, was a child of 'inexhaustible' energy and passion, brimming with confidence and courage, her teachers used to remark in her school report cards. Was perception reality? As Hae-a came into being, it was the realization of what I wished, imagined, and dreamed. While my wife was expecting twins, I named them Hae-a, 해아, in Korean alphabet meaning 'the child of the Sun' and Hae-a, 海兒 in Chinese characters meaning 'the child of the sea,' as my personal mantras for them to be 'sunny' and 'romantic.' But then they were born premature and put in incubators. One survived and the other one became the surviving twin's guardian angel.

May Hae-a. Su-a, and Song-a and everybody else sojourning on earth have no bad weather, only different kinds of good weather, rain or shine.

I traveled light right back to the future. Many moons ago, when I was working as a houseboy, my two surrogate father figures, one American and the other one British, promised to send me to the Juilliard School and to Oxford University; it was not meant to be. Even so, my two children went there instead, Hae-a to Oxford and Su-a to the Juilliard.

In September 2013, I wrote an 'Open Letter: The Sea of Cosmos,' which was sent to U.S. President Obama and Russian President Putin. The Sept. 12, 2013, Op-Ed article in The New York Times: "A Plea for Caution from Russia" by Vladimir V. Putin, president of Russia, prompted me to write this letter to all my fellow human beings all over the world.

In concluding his plea, Mr. Putin says that he carefully studied Mr. Obama's address to the nation on that Tuesday (September 10, 2013) and that he disagreed about the case President Obama put forth when he stated that the United States' policy is "what makes America different. It's what makes us [the United States] exceptional."

I, for one, concur with President Putin's apt comment that "it is extremely dangerous to encourage people to see themselves as exceptional, whatever the motivation." From time immemorial, most, if not all, human tragedies have been visited upon us, in my humble opinion, by two major mindsets: One is the self-serving "chosen-species-racist" view, and the other one is the harmful concept of "original sin" instilled in childhood.

I firmly believe in the truth that we, not only human beings, but all things in Nature are one and the same. We would have been far better off, had we been enlightened early on to realize we were related — part of each other — like the ancient aphorism: 피아일체, 'per-ah-il-che' in Korean phonetic alphabet and 彼我一體 in Chinese characters, meaning that 'we (you and I) are one and the same.' Another aphorism goes: 물아일체, 'mool-ah-il-che' in Korean phonetic alphabet and 物我一體 in Chinese characters, meaning that 'all things and I are one and the same.' Simply put, when I hurt or help you, I'm hurting or helping myself; when I destroy or divine Nature, I'm destroying or divining myself. Perhaps that's why and how it's possible that eternity consisted of a flash of a lightning-like moment when we became the very object of our love, as the German mystic Jakob Boehme (1575–1624) believed.

Let me further present my case in point. Born in now-North Korea, I happened to be in the south when the country was divided at the end of World War II, which ended the 35-year-old colonial rule of Korea by Japan; hence the Korean War in the heat of the Cold War tension and its ongoing aftermath. By virtue of serendipity and survival instinct of 'sink or swim,' I've always counted every stroke of luck as a blessing and believed nothing was to be discarded.

Eleventh of 12 children, I became fatherless at the age of five and homeless when I was fourteen, during the

Korean War. Consequently, I went on a journey, at an early age, in search of the sublime in our human condition, seeking my cosmic identity in the greater scheme of things. No matter where one is from, if we look at things from the big picture, we all are 'cosmians arainbow' passing through as fleeting sojourners on this tiny leaf-boat-like planet earth floating in the sea of cosmos.

If each one of us, be it a grain of sand, a drop of water, a blade of grass, or a human being, is indeed a micro-cosmos reflecting a macro-cosmos of all that existed in the past, all that exists in the present and all that will exist in the future, we're all in it together, all on our separate journeys to realize we must all sing the Cosmos Cantata together. No one is exceptional and all of us are exceptional.

When I was diagnosed with cancer fourteen years ago, I started to compose a short, true story of my life in the form of a fairy tale for my five daughters as my only legacy. All I wanted to say in my writings was this:

Always changing and impermanent though life is,
Troubled and sorrowful though life is,
What a blessing it is to be born than not to be born at all!
What felicity it is to love somebody,
Even if you may be crossed in love and heart-broken!
Isn't it such a beautiful, blissful, and wonderful experience to live and to love?!
By so doing we learn to fly and to soar.

And a small portion my daughter's recent eulogy to her husband reflects those sentiments:

I spoke of how ridiculously lucky I felt to have met him;
How I had no regrets about anything on our journey.
I told him that I had never sought for perfection in
anything in my life,
But that somehow I had found it;
I had found it in 'us.'
We were perfect,
Perfect in our imperfections too,
Our imperfectly perfect balance.

And Doris Wenzel, my American publisher reflected on their exceptional lives in:

To The Couple I Do Not Know

I have never met those two young people
Impressing those who know them
Inspiring those who don't.
I have never met those two young lovers
Wrapped in devotion to one another
Celebrating life alone and with others.
I have never met those two sweet souls
Securing a world of their own
While creating a lingering melody for the world.

After I learned of his (Gordon's) passing at the age of 46, I emailed the following short message to my daughter:

Dearest Su-a,

It is good to know that Gordon listened and understood what you had to say for an 'eternal' hour before he stopped breathing and he was gone so 'peacefully.'

Su-a, you are such an amazing girl. I'm even envious of you, not only for having found 'the love of your life' but more for living it to the best, to the fullest, so intensely, so poetically, very short though it was only for 13 months.

Even if one lives to be over a hundred, still it will be nothing but a breath, a droplet of waves breaking on the shore, returning to the sea of cosmos. Thus we never leave 'the sea inside.'

Love, Dad XX

Chapter X

The Eighth Lady, Arainbow

She, the Arainbow, Is Getting Arainbow

In my late forties, I came to New York, almost penniless after turning over all my assets to the mother of my children, in search of my true self. Selling wigs during the day, I was sheltered in the tiny storage space in the rear of the store at night, turning wigs into rainbows of thoughts and explored the cosmos.

'Arainbow,' this is the first tower of my thoughts. I found the path to 'truth' arainbow. Truth cannot be monopolized by religions or philosophies. It belongs to those who come into contact with it and get enlightened by it. Neither Buddha, Jesus, Muhammad, nor Socrates, Plato, Aristotle, nor Confucius, Lao Tzu, Zhuangzi own it. It applies to all beings and all things in Nature.

Among numerous paths towards 'truth,' I chose none and I decided to carve out my own. That's Arainbow! Through her I realized that I'm divine as others are. But for others, I cannot be. This fact is a matter of course but this realization is the truth. This truth manifests itself through us, not from God. What comes from "God" is false. This is how I built the tower of Arainbow, as a drop of water makes the ocean. In the deep of the night, I wandered through the night sky, treading upon stars of words, and rhapsodized about the beautiful brevity of life, without minding the divine eternity meaningless to us.

On everyone and everything that exists I conferred the title of Arainbow, not to follow but to be on the rainbow of being itself. As all human beings were born from the wombs of women, Arainbow is another name for women, who are the most mysterious and sacred saviors of humanity. Another name for Arainbow is none other than myself within myself, the essence of myself. Thus floating and flying in the sea and sky of cosmos, I brought about the Arainbow by exchanging some questions and answers as follows:

Tae-Sang (T)   Arainbow, where is the 'Heaven' we all so desire to go to?

Arainbow (A)   Tae-Sang, do you think the heaven is in the sky? If there is the God of heaven in the sky, there is the Goddess of earth in the ground. So the God of heaven and the Goddess of earth made love to each other and gave birth to the child. This child is the very heaven itself. There is no heaven in the sky and there is no hell on earth unless you make one. When you grown-up adults, adulterated by greed and stupidity, recover your childlike innocence and purity, that's your heaven. Don't waste your precious moments of life, seeking the heaven elsewhere.

T   Then how can we retain this childlike heaven?

A   In the eye of a child, all are flowers, stars, rainbows. Like children, all things in nature are pure and simple.

As children see them, everything is heaven, be it the sky, the sea, the land, the grass, the tree, or the birds. All are one and the same, you and I; humans, animals, plants and rocks; spring, summer, autumn, and winter; day and night. To a child, all is one. Oneness is the god/goddess and the heaven itself. Tae-Sang, look within, you already have the heaven.

T   Yes, you are right. God/Goddess is Oneness. The heaven is within me, as long as I retain my childhood, and the sense of wonder and mystery of it all.

A   If you can't find the heaven on earth, you can never find it anywhere else. Those who say that it's in the sky, in the universe, in the multiverse or in God, they've never seen it, not even its shadow. This planet earth itself is the God and Goddess as one, the Child, and the Heaven, all in one.

T   Seven years ago, I visited my sister Wan-Soon in L.A., California. She passed away at the age of 82. That night in my dream I saw a bird flying out of the window of her hospital room and the next day she breathed out her last breath. At that very moment she had the most peaceful face of a baby, just like what our 94-year-old mother had at the very last moment of her life.

A   All of you come and go as babies, like heaven to heaven. A child is, from the beginning to the end, peace itself, love itself, nothing else.

T   Arainbow, I was always curious, wondering about…what's life after all?

A   Nobody knows for sure. You've got to live it to know. That's all I know.

T   I, too, think so. If we could know it without living it out, it won't be life. Would it be?

A   Tae-Sang, have you ever met anyone who came out of life without dying? The constancy of inseparable birth and death, impermanence in another word, is the unchangeable fact to be accepted, like it or not. It's the same with everything else, including the cosmos. Maybe that's why American Nobel Prize winning physicist Steven Weinberg wrote in his 1977 book '*The First Three Minutes*,' "The more the universe seems comprehensible, the more it also seems pointless." By this statement, he must have meant to say that you have to make your points by how you live and love, for the universe to acquire meaning. You can take a hint from a truism that 'a traveler's writings say more about the traveler than about the place traveled to.' Or it may be as Mark Twain says in his farewell address: "Narrative should flow as flows the brook…a brook that never goes straight for a minute… Nothing to do but make the trip; how of is not important so that the trip is made."

T   Come to think of it, life may be just a concept, just like a child breaking the flower. To a child, the flower being deflowered may only be a concept, not an existing entity. Perchance only when one stops seeking the meaning of life, one can be free from the cage of living and start ascending to the sky of celestial bliss.

A   The untrodden path is always tempting and irresistible. You learn in youth and you understand in maturity. It would be wiser not to waste your allotted time puzzling over life, and instead to become an artist of life, creating a most beautiful and wonderful masterpiece of love. Tae-Sang, have you thought about me within you?

T   You and I, we both are energies. Yours are the spiritual and mines are the physical, and yet we are both sides of the same coin. If you are the sea, I am the waves. If you are the sky, I am the clouds. You are the castle of my thoughts and I'm residing in it.

A   That's right, I'm the castle of thoughts you built. Each breath of your thoughts, or each drop of your sweat, tear, and blood is all of me. The world is utterly mysterious beyond one's knowledge and imagination, and all its beauty cannot be discovered with one's intellectual eyes, but with one's eyes of wisdom just as you found me with your spiritual eyes.

T   Arainbow, let's dance. I get in the mood when I am in solitude and tranquility like now where I can feel the pulsation of the cosmos that awakens all the sensuality from each and every cell of my body. At a moment like this, how can we not dance passionately together?

A   Alright, then, dancing is an act of recalling the original spirit of the cosmos. Dancing without music is like the ocean without waves. Wind, water, flowers and stars, everything is music. Music is the rainbow flying on the wings of dancing. Two are dancing as one like us. All the sounds of the universe are moaning music. Therefore, music is another word for love. Sounds are the rhythm and melodies of Nature.

T   To tell you the truth, Arainbow, ever since my youngest days, I've been obsessed with music, all kinds of music that is.

Music, 음악 in Korean phonetic alphabet, and 音樂 in two Chinese characters, meaning the pleasure of sound, can also at the same time mean with another Chinese character used 淫樂 — instead of 音樂 — carnality. So quite interestingly enough, music in Korean means 'the erotic pleasure' as well as 'the pleasure of sound.' This is a case of homonym in English. Coincidentally, there is another case of almost homonym in English, too— organism and orgasm.

Listen to this little poem I composed in my childhood. A poem becomes a song. A song becomes a wind. A wind becomes a boat sailing in the sea of cosmos. This poem is passing through us at this very moment. Let's sing it together.

'Zol zol zol zol zol'
The sound of the brook
Trickling to the sea

'Salrang, salrang'
The breathing sound of love
Going in and coming out

'Sswa sswa'
The melody of the wind
Blowing up the sky

'Choolrung choolrung'
The rhythm of dancing
Of spring flowers
Under the autumn moon

'Chulsok chulsok'
The screams of waves
Crashing on the rock

'Ttock ttock'
The pattering of raindrops
Kissing the flowers

'Kkoekkol kkoekkol'
The song of Orioles
On the spring branches of the tree

'Gaegul gaegul'
Croaking of the toads
In the summer pond

'Guittle guittle'
Singing of the crickets
From the autumn brushes
In the night

'Booung Booung'
The love calls of the owl
In the winter mountains

A   Music is a synonym of breath. It causes infinitely mysterious and wonderful waves between in-breaths and out-breaths. Music is the live organism. All Music is unique. There are no two of the same. Heaven and earth, men and women, animals and plants, all, dancing to the music of love, perpetuate the circle of life.

T   Arainbow, is music made of inspiration?

A   Music, I think, is rather seeking out the same sort of energy from all the energies. Wouldn't it be pushing and pulling of energies, as light is separated from darkness, like the moon waxes and wanes? We are moved by music because, of all the senses, our hearing is most keenly connected to the cosmos. There must be some secret, mystical link between the wavelengths of music and the cosmic structure.

T   Arainbow, didn't you come to me in a wave of music? Ha-ha—

A   May it be so! My eye twitching or rather my subtle inner body tremor might have reached out and got in touch with your energies. The stone of sound thrown in my pond of passion must have caused a stir and the energy of vibrating ripples awakened me. Thus we've pulled and embraced each other for the erections in our musical bodies, for sure.

T   Oh, what a cool confession! If so, we've found the cosmos in chaos; it was inevitable, not a coincidence. Mysteriously, it wouldn't be wrong for me to say that if you were the organism, I would be the orgasm. Would it be?

A   Ho ho, woah, let's sing and dance, celebrating life. As music and dancing are one, so are we, you and me. Let's dance to the music of Nature. Tae-Sang, I composed a poem for you:

You and me
All of us two together
Heaven and earth
Yin and yang
Man and woman
Male and female
Mountain and valley
Let's dance all together
To the music of love
Enjoying the pleasures of
Sensuality and spirituality of
Both chaos and cosmos
Cheers to us!

T   I'll cherish this poem for eternity. Now I'd like to share with you, Arainbow, two perfect songs for us: '*The Power of Love*,' as sung by German singer Helene Fisher and '*Wind Song*' as sung by Korean singer Son Seung-yeon with its refrain *"I will love everything in this world."*

T   Now I'd like to talk about a mundane issue, namely about money. Didn't Roman philosopher Seneca say that 'wealth is the slave of a wise man, the master of a fool?'

A   People worship money. If money is God, what are you humans? In India, where conflicts between material wealth and dearth exist, life is the sea of Truth, Dharma and Karma, and the ultimate goal of life is Moksha (Nirvana) to the Hindus. It's the same everywhere, not only in India. Isn't it?

T   Arainbow, let me tell you about my sister Tae-Soon, who was two years older than me. Thirty-seven years ago, she lost her life at the age of 48 due to the wealth she acquired.

A   Yes, indeed, money can corrupt you, whereas love purifies you. Tell me now what happened to your dear sister Tae-Soon, Tae-Sang.

T   There's 'The Pearl,' a novella by American writer John Steinbeck, first published in 1947. It is a story (later made into a movie) of a pearl diver, Kino, and explores man's nature, as well as greed, defiance of societal norms, and evil. Tae-Soon's story is a classic example of The Pearl made in the real life.

Tae-Soon married an American scholar of East Asian Studies. He was fluent in Chinese, Japanese, and Korean, taught at several American universities and wrote history books about Korea.

Assisting in research works for her husband, raising two sons and editing and publishing 'EVERYDAY KOREAN: A Basic English-Korean Wordbook,' Tae-Soon became a realtor. She was very successful, earning much more money than her husband. Either feeling diminished, or gripped by greed, her husband also became a real estate broker, and they founded a real estate company. He managed the office work and Tae-Soon did all the fieldwork, leading a group of over 50 agents under her supervision.

When my family went to Hawaii from England in 1978 at their invitation for me to join Tae-Soon in her business, she told me about the secret of her success as a salesperson: 'Talk Less; Listen More; Make Sure You

Are 100% Satisfied as Buyer.' In other words: 'Never, Never Push.' If the prospective buyer is satisfied only 99%, the deal will fall through sooner or later.

In due course, my sister and her husband became almost billionaires, but alas, he started womanizing and indulging in high stakes gambling. Despairing about the chances of his returning to his senses, Tae-Soon divorced him, giving away most of their assets. In a few years, he squandered his share and was practically a penniless, homeless guy. Taking pity on him, she took him in as a lodger, not as husband again but as the father of the children.

Early one morning, she drove up a hill on a dirt road for a listing of a mansion being built on top the hill after dropping off the kids at Punahou School, the private school former U.S. President Obama attended. In the afternoon, her body was discovered, apparently run over by the car she was driving.

We were then back in England for our children to attend the Chetham's School of Music in Manchester. One night in my dream I saw the scene of an accident. The next day, I received a telegram. I thought it was about our mother passing away, as she was living with Tae-Soon. To my great surprise, it was about the accident involving Tae-Soon. She left a will, leaving everything to the children, but since they were still minors, their father must have received her assets. He died of a heart attack ten years later.

So, Arainbow, don't you think this elegy can serve as a dire warning for the living about 'curses in disguise?' I might tell you, Arainbow, about another weird dream I had, about my brother Myung-Sang, who was ten years older than me. Again, while we were living in England, in my dream one night he came and went without saying much as usual. The next day, I got the news that he passed away. It must have been a 'goodbye' from him in my dream.

Myung-Sang dropped out of school in his adolescence and went on a life-long journey, seeking after 'the way' or 'the truth,' whatever it might mean. From then on, he was never concerned what to wear, what to eat, or how to make a living. He wandered around the country, always on foot, visiting different spiritual teachers and reading books about different philosophies and religions of the world. He stayed in caves of the mountains, for days, meditating and nibbling uncooked grains and pine nuts. Like a tramp, he was dressed in rags with his hair grown long, a disgrace to his family.

To his widowed mother, he was simply a crazy and lazy bum, irresponsible to no end but not quite irredeemable. So she got him married so he could have a family and wake up to reality on earth, off from his highfalutin mumbo jumbo, once and for all. But it was to no avail, and he was a vagabond all the same, spreading words of love and peace. Although he was written off as good-for-nothing bum by his family, he was regarded by some people as a guru and a healer. He was even credited for having cured some incurable, by prescribing herbal medicine, such as pine needles brewed in honeyed water for coughing, asthma, pneumonia, and tuberculosis. But he was saying that whatever he suggested worked only for those who believed in its efficacy, and that our body has the built-in self-healing mechanism.

Although he was deemed and dismissed as insane, I was curious about what he was saying about many things, especially about 'chukjipob 一 축지법' in Korean alphabet and 縮地法 in Chinese characters, 'a method of making a long distance close in by the magic of contracting space.' One day, I asked him how I could do it. He took me to a small brook. Holding his hand as I walked backward from the water, the width of the stream grew narrower to the point of appearing to be a silvery line. Then I was told to run toward the edge of the water, and then to jump. He forewarned me that as I came to closer to the water, its width would look wider. "Don't look at the widening stream of water. If you just fix the image of that silvery line in your head and focus on it, you can easily jump over the brook."

Once he was debating metaphysical issues with top-ranking Buddhist monks at Jogyesa, the head temple of Korea. When they got to the point beyond which they couldn't discuss further with words, he politely asked one of the monks to fetch a gourd-full of night soil from the outhouses. When his request was obliged, he swallowed it to the last drop. All those Buddhists were reminded of the well-known episode of Wonhyo, I was told later by one of those monks who had participated in the debate. The story *Water in a Skull* goes like this:

About fourteen hundred years ago, there was a famous monk named Wonhyo (617-686) in Korea. He thought he would become a better monk if went to

China to attain more knowledge about Buddhism. He embarked on a long journey to China with his fellow seeker/student, Euisang.

He continued his journey on foot and, one day, he was passing through one region in Baekje (one of the three kingdoms: Koguryo in the north, Baekje in the middle and Silla in the south of the peninsula). They faced heavy rain, so they sought some shelter. They took shelter in a very safe-looking cave and decided to stay the night inside the cave.

While he was sleeping, Wonhyo woke up and felt extremely thirsty. He was searching, in the darkness, for something to drink. He found water in a gourd and drank it without hesitation. The water was cool and refreshing, and quenched his thirst. He fell asleep again.

Next morning, Wonhyo and Euisang woke up and were frightened by the skulls scattered around them. The shelter they had spent one night in was not a cave but an old grave. Also, Wonhyo realized that the fresh water in the gourd that quenched his thirst was actually some stagnant water in a skull. The moment he realized this, he threw up.

Through this experience, Wonhyo attained a big enlightenment about how important one's mind was. He then reflected and realized that he had been trying to become a good monk by attaining more knowledge about Buddhism. Wonhyo then cancelled his plan to study in China and abandoned his position as a monk. He became a laity again and reverentially devoted himself to meditation throughout his entire life. He gave inspiration to many laity.

Arainbow, don't you think my brother Myung-Sang paraphrased by his action, not in words, what William Shakespeare said?

There is nothing either clean (good) or dirty (bad) but thinking makes it so?

T   Arainbow, I should add that no matter how ill-treated by some people, I have never seen my brother Myung-Sang speak ill of anybody. I believe that he literally practiced all his life this famous phrase: *"With malice toward none, with charity for all,"* as quoted from Abraham Lincoln's second inaugural address. One thing I still cannot comprehend by any sense and wits is how he could have predicted the outbreak of the war exactly one year ahead of time. One day he came to our mother to tell her to stock up some extra supply of provisions in preparation for the hard times to face. After dismissing his warning as a 'madman talk,' she nevertheless prepared just in case. We were surprised that it indeed did happen as he had pre-warned. What would you say about this? Was it a kind of prophecy, or a case of clairvoyance?

A   Tae-Sang, you must understand, stand under, or underlook, look under, to realize there are much more than what's audible, tangible, and visible to our senses. You may call them supernatural phenomena, but they are really and truly extra, or rather ultra-scheme of things. Mind you, there's the first principle of the so-called General Semantics: Nobody knows everything about anything.

T	One day, while clearing a blocked gutter under the edge of the roof of my house in a suburb of London, I found something strange growing there. I couldn't tell if they were plants or mineral deposits. They were hard, in the shape of tiny stars; strange objects of curiosity, wonder and mystery. I gave some of them to my children so that they could show them to their teachers and friends. Whatever their substance might have been, I thought, they must have come to bear an uncanny resemblance to the stars. They were singing and whispering through night and day. It recalled a fairy tale of a hunchback Persian princess who became straight and tall by stretching herself daily in front of her straight-backed statue. I had a sudden awakening to the natural phenomena common everywhere, in the air, on land and beneath the ocean, with sunflowers and starfish serving as constant reminders. We all know that sunflowers look for the sunlight. But what I didn't know was that on a cloudy day, they looked at each other, looking for the energy they give one another, standing high and tall. How better it would be, if humans could do the same!

One summer day, years ago, my family vacationed in the Caribbean. Early one morning, I went out for a walk on the shore. It just so happened that I spotted a tropical fish jumping up and down, unable to return to the water after the ebb tide. I quickly scooped the fish up in my two hands formed into a bowl and let it go back to the sea. The next morning, I found a beautiful conch shell at the same spot where I'd rescued the fish. To me, the conch shell seemed to be a 'thank-you gift' from the fish.

As someone once said, 'to be certain about anything in life was the privilege of a fool, because there was only one thing to be certain about: that there was nothing to be certain of.'

What decided how you started in life and how you developed? Was it happenstance or heavenly providence? Be that as it may, there is no denying that you are a product of birth and circumstance. If you were eagle-born, how could you laugh at a snail for being so low and slow? It might have been possible that the snail dying to be an eagle became a frog after trying so hard for so long, just as animals wishing to be godlike developed into humans.

Yes, Arainbow, there's our 'froglike' self-portrait. I can't recall whether I saw this lyrically unflattering and ungrammatical portrait, drawn by somebody, of humans from the swamplands in a dream or in my waking hours:

What a wonderful bird
The frog are!
When he stand, he sits
Almost.
When he hops he fly almost.
He ain't got no sense hardly,
He ain't got no tail hardly,
Either.
When he sit, he sit on what
He ain't got, almost.

Arainbow, when I first read this famous poem *"The Rainbow"* (1802) as a boy, I felt my own soliloquy was voiced by a kindred spirit by the name of William Wordsworth (1770–1850), the celebrated English poet laureate, about one hundred fifty years earlier.

My Heart Leaps Up

My heart leaps up,
When I behold
A rainbow in the sky;
So was it when I was a Child,
So is it now I am a Man,
So be it when I shall grow old,
Or let me die!
The Child is Father of the Man;
And I could wish my days to be
Bound each to each
By natural piety.

Truth to tell, Arainbow, I wasn't satisfied with this poem, just looking up to behold a rainbow in the sky. So I created you to be right on The Rainbow, 'upgressing,' or rather ascending on top of the rainbow. Hence, you were borne of me!

A   Tae-Sang, let me now ask you about sex. What do you get from sex? What's sex to you?

T   I think sex is the best thing the divine Cosmos gave us. If we look at sex as a means just for reproduction, it doesn't mean much. I used to blame the Creator for not having designed us so as to make sex possible only between two lovers, and only through this union could a baby be born as the fruition of true love. Then there wouldn't have been prostitution, rape, and divorce. But come to think of it further, had it been so, then one couldn't have the suspense and thrill of seeking the love of one's life, without which life would be so boring and empty. I've come to the conclusion that life was far better as it was.

A Yes, indeed, of course, why not? Sex is the most urgent and desperate ode to life, braving death. From the purely biological perspective, libido is everything about sex—whereby the ultimate happiness and joy of creating posterity are achieved. Libido is stronger and much more powerful than death. Otherwise, how could there be praying mantises and black widow spiders? It's only natural, regardless of species, that all females pick and choose alpha males for superior genes.

T Isn't sex nothing to be ashamed of? A lot of people seem to have been brainwashed and the indoctrinated 'puritanical' mindset set in for them to regard sex as 'dirty.' What a 'constipational' conspiracy of twisted thoughts full of hideous hypocrisy! Let's imagine, Arainbow, you and I are having sex. How breathtakingly beautiful, how intrinsically intimate, how inspiring and uplifting, how mysteriously magical, how naturally nirvanic, how secret and sacred it is! Isn't it, Arainbow? Without making love by having sex, the world will be just chaos, ruled by the law of the jungle and the survival of the fittest, where there is no aurora, nor rainbow. Isn't the breathing body that knows no love but a zombie? So I couldn't help agreeing more with the German-American poet Charles Bukowski (1920–1994) when he wrote, "Sex is kicking death in the ass while singing."

A   Sex is neither good nor bad. It's the cosmos created out of the chaos by the union of body and soul, the cosmic matter and mind merged into one. This is Cosmos Cantata.

T   Now that my life is coming to an end, how can I unriddle death?

A   No doubt death is the toughest riddle. So far, nobody has yet solved or deciphered this enigmatic mystery of death, either philosophically or scientifically. If you define death as the end of life, the total and permanent cessation of the vital functions of an organism, then what is life? Without defining life first, one cannot define death. Could you?

T   Didn't Confucius say: "if we don't know life, how can we know death?"

A   So true! One can say only as much or as little as one loves life, or rather as much or as little as one lives to love anybody or anything at all.

T   Maybe we were born to die. Then to die well is to live well. Won't it, Arainbow?

A   If the universe existing and moving as programmed by the Great Designer is as honest and simple as an idiot or a robot, then life and death are no different. Leonardo da Vinci was quoted as saying that, "While I thought I was learning how to live, I have been learning how to die." Didn't Kahlil Gibran remind you? "For life and death are one, even as the river and the sea are one." The famous Korean Buddhist thinker Wonhyo, whom you mentioned earlier, is said to have pointed out the fact that as death was pain, so was birth. I don't agree with this perception, that both birth and death are sufferings. Life and death are the natural processes of your cosmic journey, the most amazing and wonderful gift of blessings granted you.

T We have a saying in Korea, that 'a live dog is better than a dead tiger.' This expresses our strong attachment to life, taking death as the most terrorizing act of coup de grace administered to life.

A If it's a divine punishment to die when it's time for you to live, so must it be to live when it's time for you to die, as another saying goes. People believe in religions for fear of death. But if you go by the 'law of energy conservation,' the energies of body will go on to exist somehow, one way or other, in the universe after they expire from the body full of energy when it was breathing. Therefore, there is nothing for you to fear or worry about, I can assure you.

T Ah, then, overcoming the fear of death as de-existing and turning into 'nothing' must be the crux of the matter. And then one can look forward hopefully to continuing one's unforeseeable and unpredictable cosmic journey through other planets and stars of different galaxies and universes or multiverses. In other words, it must be changing one's attitudes and perspectives. Is that what you mean?

A Yes, that's correct. You cannot attain perfection and eternity with your body. Material matters always change forms, say like ice, water, and vapor, and they vary in shapes like clouds in the sky. That's the true state of affairs. So you just live your life from birth to death as a drop of water trickles into the sea of cosmos. As the changing seasons of spring, summer, autumn and winter, there are different seasons of life: birth, infancy, childhood, adolescence, youth, middle age, old age, and death; singing songs of birth and death, songs of joy and sorrow—you have to find the divine and the eternal in yourself. That's what all of you, or rather all of us are.

Chapter XI

The Ninth Lady, Cosmian
She, the Cosmian, Is on a Cosmic Journey

I sold my wig store in New Jersey and became a court interpreter in New York. I began to interpret things through a kaleidoscope of variegated colors and creeds of humanity, either prescribed or proscribed by all kinds of custom, dogma, law, and regulation. As I started to see things from the cosmic perspective, I've come to realize that we all were Cosmians on our cosmic journeys arainbow.

A Cosmian is no avatar of the Cosmos, but the Cosmos itself. All things are made of cells, molecules, and particles of love. So is the fact that flowers are blooming; stars are twinkling; and that I am loving you, whatever or whoever you are.

All synonyms of love are Cosmian. So is life free of delusions and illusions. A Cosmian is shackled neither by obsessions nor by possessions, neither by pleasures nor by pains of any sort. A Cosmian loves both life and death, in joy and sorrow as one.

I invited all the ladies who helped me to find and fulfill myself to the Cosmian Festival I'm hosting tonight. They are my dear Cosmians. They are my Goddesses, the Maestras of Life laboring in the Magic and Miracle of Love.

First to arrive was the Mother, followed by the Athena, the Truth/Goodness/Beauty, the Cosmos, the Chaos, the United Kingdom, the Child, the Arainbow, and the Cosmian.

Sitting at the round table and drinking tea, we were admiring all the beauty of the world one cares to behold. All excited, my suddenly reawakened, rejuvenated and revitalized libido jumped out of me and was swimming through the sea of stardust in their eyes to pick their cherries ripened on their sweet lips. The words we're going to share will become scintillating stars in the dark sky.

Tae-Sang (T)   Thank you, my dearest Ladies, for coming across time and space. Let's freely talk about anything, without restraints and taboos.

Athena (At)   Speaking for all of us here, thank you, Tae-Sang, for your invitation.

T   People are anxious to get to their destinations without knowing where they are heading for.

United Kingdom (UK) Those who know their destinations are the awakened ones. In order to be aware of what's happening, one has to find one's true identity and purpose.

Chaos (Ch) If misdirected, how fast and how far you go is pointless, isn't it?

Cosmos (C)   Apart from metaphysical issues, what about all the mundane affairs, which are nothing short of warfare hell-bent on winning?

Truth/Goodness/Beauty (TGB) As you know, Cosmos, people are eager to sell their souls for the ephemeral, evanescent, mirage-like fortunes of fame, money, and power.

As we went on, the cool evening breeze was dancing and caressing the ladies getting warm by the interesting subjects:

Mother (M)   The world is a battleground where people fight for greed, not for hunger.

Arainbow (A) But if it wasn't for greed, evolution would not have happened.

Cosmian (Cn) People are foolhardy to make life so difficult and miserable by becoming so heavy-hearted and too serious about every little thing. It's like being penny-wise and pound-foolish. Isn't it?

M   The thing is, that people make problems and troubles where there are none. Life is a great feast to enjoy, singing and dancing to the music of the Cosmos.

At   As John Lennon and Yoko Ono demonstrated by their performance art in order to get their urgent message of the song *Imagine* get across, how different life would be for everybody and everything if we just made love, not war, like bonobos. But, alas, look at me. I would not have come into being if there were no wars.

T   As Jawaharlal Nehru was quoted as saying: "The only alternative to coexistence is co-destruction." Nevertheless, even war-making may be the process of progressing from Chaos to Cosmos. In the final analysis, predators and preys are serving the same

113

purpose complementing each other to make everything perfect, methinks.

Ch People prefer being born princes or princesses to building one's own world. You can turn a misfortune into a fortune, making a cosmos out of chaos or vice versa. The point is that wherever you go, it will be a heaven with love, but a hell without love, depending on whether you are on the same or different wavelength, so to speak.

UK As you all know, I have been at the pinnacle of world power. That's how I know how sweet and addictive are the temptations of dominance, a life of privilege and wealth, a sense of chosen species. The British Empire was built by piracy all over the world, in accordance with the law of the jungle and the natural principle of survival of the fittest.

TGB Even so, thank heaven and earth, it's the privilege of humans to seek endlessly the truth, goodness and beauty.

C People look down on prostitutes but wasn't Mary Magdalene a friend of Jesus? When you think about it, as 'comfort women,' they provide far more beneficial, charitable services of mercy, when they embrace men as mothers hold babies in their arms. They take a pittance and give the great pleasure, whereas mercenaries and soldiers give pain and take lives. Let's compare them with all the high-priced, sacred and noble, and looked-up-to people: clerics, lawyers, physicians, and politician, prostituting themselves in the name of God, Law, Medicine, and Patriotism.

Thus saying, sipping jasmine tea, the Cosmos was commiserating with all the slaves of sex, housekeeping, and childcare of the world, and all the other ladies nodded in unison.

T   That's why I, too, have come to abhor, detest, and deplore the male biology of violence and war, while admiring, adoring, and idolizing the female chemistry of love and peace.

Child (Cd) I think love is life, no matter whether it's a prostitute's physical love or a nun's spiritual love. Love as life is the everlasting light, the source of all that is noblest, purest, the most beautiful in human life, the perfect organism/orgasm, that is.

Cosmian (Cn) True! Love is manna fallen from the Cosmos. I want to share this crucial, the most essential, food with all the dying of hunger. In a grain of rice, therein lies all the energy and ether of soil, sun, and wind grown by the drops of toiling farmer's sweat. So partaking of a meal is participation in the order and providence of the Cosmos. And an act of eating is an awakening as well as a metaphor.

T   Dearest Mother, I'm the fruit of your love, soaked in your blood, sweat, and tear. I worship all the mothers of the world with my deepest gratitude.

At   I doubt if all the mothers of the world deserve to be worshipped. The so-called Mother Nature is not a matter of course, and it shouldn't be taken for granted.

A   This is really shocking that there is no natural Mother Nature. If Mother Nature is an innate instinct, wouldn't it be only natural, Athena?

At That Mother Nature is an instinct that makes anything possible, and that motherhood must be borne by all women at any cost, is the most outrageous anachronism of today. It cannot be imposed and forced upon women any longer. It is sheer terrorism committed against women. It's long past time to make a transition from the instinctive to the subjective motherhood. Don't you agree?

Ch Nowadays, many girls nip the bud of Mother Nature before it gets fully developed by giving up on getting married to have children. It's a matter of choice, not a pre-destined and pre-ordained obligation or mission to be accomplished at all costs.

Cd I do agree. There are some girls, like myself, who can't and won't go all-in into motherhood. I'd rather put a period to the hereditary cloning of my DNA, in order to enjoy my carefree single life. This is my way of loving myself.

Cn The dogma of the Mother Nature's indisputability is fascism. When you get over this socially indoctrinated motherhood, your own subjective Mother Nature will develop naturally.

T   Mother Nature and women are such interesting and mysterious subjects we can go on discussing endlessly.

Cd I haven't given birth to a child. I don't welcome the propagation of humanity, because I deplore the appalling reality that humans have been destroying the natural order of the Cosmos, polluting the air, water and everything else of Nature. What am I? Come to think of it, am I not nothing more or nothing less than a gene pouch generated by the union of my father's sperm and my mother's egg? We've had enough of the gene reproduction. Hahaha.

M Oh, my good heaven and earth's sake, what a different world it is now! It's no more matter of fact that all girls must get married and have children to raise. It's awful and awesome at the same time.

UK Mother Nature is the same regardless of the East or of the West. Its subject is woman and its object is her child. But for the Mother Nature, human evolution would have been discontinued. Think about the British Royal Family, for example. Diana missed it since she became motherless early in her life.

C What an unlucky poor girl she was!

UK On top of that, she was not happy after she married 12-year-older Prince Charles, as her husband carried on an extramarital affair with his first love, who was older than him. Like a child, he sought a mother-like love from this woman whom he married after Diana died so tragically.

TGB Mothers are the eternal objects of all longings. So was it, no doubt, for Princess Diana and Prince Charles.

UK Mother is the safest haven for a child. Camilla Parker Bowles (Camilla, Duchess of Cornwall) must have been providing the mother-like love that Prince Charles craved. Diana's son Prince Harry, too, confessed that there was never a day when he didn't miss his mother.

117

T	I guess that's why I keep warning young girls that when they marry a man, they'll be adopting a child, the youngest one at that.

Our conversation at dinner table went on endlessly. Of course, these ladies had no substance, and had only concept. They were only fictional phantom characters, none other than my alter egos, whom I invited to this final party of ours.

C	Let's change the subject now and talk about parting when this party is going to be over, sadly.

Ch	Meeting and parting, life and death, cosmos and chaos are inseparable, like Siamese twins.

M	As flowers bloom and fall, humans are born and die. But don't say it is sadness. It's more like breathing in and breathing out. Think about it. How can breathing go on without in and out? Imagine birth without death. Imagine one is young and lives forever. That wouldn't be being young and living. A picnic that never ends is no picnic at all. Would it?

UK	Were it not for farewells or passing away, God might not have been invented by humans.

Cd	Saying goodbye is the most painful and saddest feeling I experienced when I lost my husband five months after our wedding.

At	This may sound heartless. But as Rumi said: "Goodbyes are only for those who love with their eyes. Because for those who love with heart and soul there is no such thing as separation."

TGB   As Jean Paul Richter put it, "Man's feelings are always purest and most glowing in the hour of meeting and of farewell."

T   Wouldn't it depend on who feels what? Let me tell you what I learned early on. When I first started learning English in my first year of middle school (7th grade), I came across two contradictory sayings. One was 'out of sight, out of mind.' The other one was: 'Absence makes the heart grow fonder.' If both are true, I wondered, which one will apply to which circumstance. After much agonizing meditation, I came to the conclusion. If you liked mainly a person's lower half, the former applied, while if you were really in love with a person's upper half, the latter would stand. My reasoning was that a person's one and only, unique character and personality was irreplaceable whilst a person's biological anatomy could easily be available.

Ch   Now, then, what is death?

A   Not only human but all beings are mortal, or rather Cosmians afoot for a cosmic journey, afloat and aflight, arainbow, I reassure you all, my fellow mortals.

T   My dear Spanish friend from Colombia Rafael Fortich, who served as my oracle, recited this verse for me: *"I only want you to know that every action elicits a reaction, then nothing is a coincidence in this life of the Cosmos, in which we are like barges at the mercy of the storm; hence we should grab the great mast of love not to fall into the pit of nothingness."*

TGB Gabriela Mistral spoke for me when she wrote this verse: "You shall create beauty not to excite the senses but to give sustenance to the soul."

M It's better to care about life than to fear death? Living because you cannot die destroys your soul. There's no point in living without will and enthusiasm.

T In my youth, broken-hearted, I confronted death. Taking one's own life is uncalled for and undesirable, so unnatural, but a natural death is a blessing. Without death there is no life to love and enjoy. Because of death, the adventure of life is possible, so is the adventure of all adventures, the magical and mysterious miracle of love.

UK If birth is happiness, so is death. For the beginning and the end are the same.

Cn Only if you change your way of thinking so that you and the Cosmos become one, then as birth is a feast, so is death. Why worry, when I'm the Cosmos itself, even if I die.

I took out some rice wine from the fridge. Although I quit drinking a long time ago, tonight I wanted to have a drink, as this was the last supper with my ladies.

UK Now let's talk about systems. Would capitalism and communism, or democracy and socialism be the best systems humans created? Wouldn't be there any better ones? Perhaps these systems are like clothes that fit somewhat better than others.

A There is no perfect system on earth. Since no humans are perfect, how could there be perfect systems? If only the Nature is perfect as it is, then humans are perfect too, because humans are part of the Nature. If so, then, aren't humans like robots and isn't life unbearably boring? Maybe that's why humans are born perfectly imperfect so that it's up to each and every one of them either to upgrade oneself to become divine or to downgrade oneself to become beastly.

T   From early on, I judged that humans are hybrids between the divine and the beastly. If the divine resides in the heaven and the beastly dwells on earth, where should humans live, I wondered. There is infinite distance between the ideal and the reality. The heaven cannot be the earth, nor can the earth be the heaven. All humans have to keep their feet on earth since they cannot ignore or transcend the reality. And yet, they must look up, connecting to the sky, though grounded to Gaia (Mother Earth). The ideal is not meant to be achieved, I gather. Once achieved, it's no longer an ideal but a reality; hence we should strive forever for perfection. This was the path for the human beings, I decided. Any human who realizes this premise will be living the life of the enlightened.

Ch   The best fit for humans are their birthday suits. Have you seen animals, plants, or rocks wearing clothes? All the creatures lived as they were born. That's their natural systems?

Cd   Like myself, all the children of the Cosmos are unencumbered by any kind of systems or doctrines whatsoever, as free as a bird, as light as a feather, like a wind.

Cn Weren't all the free spirits like Buddha and Jesus breakers of all the fossilized sacred icons and systems of caste, family, marriage, state, synagogue, temple, and what not?

C   Love alone going beyond any kind of boundary unites with all, no matter what.

UK A classic case in point in literature is Romeo and Juliet. Another in history is Duke of Windsor and Mrs. Simpson. Some people may dismiss them as 'crazies,' captives of passion, or rather slaves of romance, intoxicated in love.

T   People are addicted to alcohol, drugs, gambling, sex, sports, if not to fame, money, and power. Some people are Allah/Jesus/Jehovah/God-intoxicated. Aren't they? If you are crazy about these things, they can corrupt you and ruin your lives. But, mind you, only love purifies and uplifts us all to become Cosmians Arainbow.

Wonhyo warned: "Do not be born, for dying is painful." I disagree. I would say: "Be born. Life is joyful. Die. To be born anew is wonderful."

Buddha bespoke that life is a bitter sea, because of birth, aging, sickness, and death; on account of happiness, anger, sorrow, and pleasure. As for me, owing to all of them, life is all the more enjoyable, far more interesting, and intriguing.

This is the Cosmian Song I've been singing all my life.

Cosmos

When I was a boy,
I liked the cosmos,
Cozy and coy
Without rhyme or reason to toss.
Later on as a young man,
I fell in love with the cosmos,
Conscious of the significance
Of this flower for me sure,
The symbol of a girl's love pure.
As I cut my wisdom teeth,
I took the Cosmian path,
Traveling the world far and near
In my pursuit of cosmos
In a chaotic world.
Upon looking back one day,
Forever longing, forever young,
Never aging and never exhausted
By yearning for cosmos,
I'd found unawares numerous cosmos
That had blossomed all along the road
That I had journeyed.
A dreamland of the bluebird,
Looking for a rainbow,
Where could it be?
Over and beyond the stormy clouds,
Lo and behold, there it is,
The wild blue yonder
Where you can sail and soar
In the sea and sky of cosmos

Arainbow, chanting Cosmos Cantata:
All's beautiful!
All's well!
All's wonderful!

We've had the most amazing party, and the ladies returned across time and space to the Cosmos. It was the greatest fortune for me to meet them. Thanks to them, I could enjoy this adventure of my life full of the mythical miracles of love and wonder.

Chapter XII
Saudade for S(e)oul

My nostalgic time travel was interrupted by the announcement that the airplane will be landing at the Incheon Airport of Seoul after a 15-hour flight.

Suddenly, Julio Iglesias' "A Song to Galicia" (1972, when I left Seoul) filled my heart:

Now that all my 11 siblings are gone, I'm the only one left treading this father/motherland of ours. Now, it's my favorite season autumn here in Korea. Wherever you go, you are greeted by cosmos flowers all along the country roads.

I began to recite this poem I composed in my adolescence:

Autumn leaves are falling

I've been traveling far away from home.
Autumn leaves tinted in yellow and red
Are falling in my pining heart bruised black and blue.

Prince and pauper,
Princess and harlot,
Father and mother,
Brothers and sisters,
Friends and neighbors,
All are falling one by one
From the tree branches of life.

Soon it'll be my turn to fall.
Before then I've got to go home
To fall fast asleep like a baby
Deep in peace in the bosom of Mother Earth.

As I realize it was only a dream
When I wake up in the morning,
I'll be realizing life too was but a dream,
When I wake up from life, dreaming.

If so, while breathing and dreaming,
Shall I sing like a bird to raise a wind
To dance with trees and grasses of
The mountains and streams of the valleys?

If so, while breathing and dreaming,
Shall I croak like a frog for rain
To cleanse the earth of all the dirty and ugly things
With the teardrops of the heaven?

If so, while breathing and dreaming,
Shall I stretch out stalks like a snail
To measure up inch by inch the height of

The sky and the size of the earth?

Or shall I listen to the song of
The waves like a conch shell?
Nah, like a bee, I'd rather call on beautiful flowers
And dream sweet dreams, collecting the honey of love.

I came here on earth uninvited and lived as my heart beat, always drunk on love. Every breath I breathed was a miracle, believing that one human moment was much more worthwhile than the divine eternity meaningless to mortals. Life is not so serious, and yet full of mystery and wonder. I was so happy with a whiff of wind, a ray of sunshine, a child's laughter, and everything of the world as anything was better than nothing.

I came to meet the ladies, but I didn't know where they were. If you ask me if they exist, I cannot say they do. If you ask me if they don't exist, I cannot say they don't. They are here and they are not here. They are the whole as one. You know that silence is the sound of time passing. Don't you? They may be passing in silence, in and out of time. So please don't ask me about the ladies. They are Cosmians Arainbow. For all of you, living here and now, are very Cosmians.

Thus, as a Cosmian myself, my cosmic journey is open-ended.

* * * * *

Endnote

In Korean singer Kim Soo-hee's hit song, *Sad Love*, the refrain is *"Why am I being diminished when I stand before you?"*

Let's apply this question to all kinds of prizes, including the Nobel Prizes. Many publishers, writers, and readers, were reported to have been greatly disappointed by the earlier news that there would be no Nobel Prize for Literature to be awarded in 2018. I was prompted by this little brouhaha to think about prizes in earnest.

Whatever the presents or the prizes might be, wasn't it much more gratifying to give them than to receive them? Come to think of it, giving them out to somebody is really giving them to oneself. Isn't it?

Whoever your sweetheart is, be it your parents, siblings, friends, lovers, spouses, children, or grandchildren, if you've ever really loved someone with all your heart and soul, you'd rather bear all the burden yourself to alleviate it from your loved one whom you could never love enough.

Be that as it may, your self-worth and *raison d'être* is not validated only when you are nominated for, or presented with a prize. Is it?

This is the case, no matter how great they may be. For example, all works of art are nothing more than imitations of nature and life. How could we then value the shadow more than the real thing?

Furthermore, nobody knows for sure whether there is such a thing called God or not. Even if such a divine super being does indeed exist, nobody is sure whether it's male, female, neuter, asexual, or whatever. How is it then possible to say anything definitive about such an unknown and unknowable being?

Similarly, how could one worship such an unreal phantom-like being—indoctrinated as all-knowing, all-mighty, all-present, all-self-righteous—while failing to love and serve all things of the Cosmos, including oneself, from the moment, to the moment and in the moment?

It behooves us then to mind our immediate business of learning diligently as life-long students of the School of Love. Thus, enlightened altogether, we may all graduate to become Cosmians Arainbow.

Afternote

Life is fulfilled every moment
when it is lived in love.

Life is totally wasted
when it's written about
without living it.

This is
not my case,
I pray.